A Town Called Seaside

A Town Called Seaside

Gloria Stiger Linkey

Cover photograph Jo Ann Danton
Published by Seacove Publishers, Seaside, Oregon 97138
@ 2016 by Gloria Stiger Linkey

ISBN: 1537320777
ISBN 13: 9781537320779
Library of Congress Control Number: 2016914491
CreateSpace Independent Publishing Platform
North Charleston, South Carolina

Dedication

This book is dedicated to my two lovely daughters, Victoria and Darci, and to my sister, Patricia. To the memory of my parents, Ray and Lydia Stiger, who raised me with such love and devotion. To all of my friends in Seaside.

Acknowledgments

————

MY DEEPEST APPRECIATION GOES TO all who assisted with this book. Mary Blake, Mary Cornell, Larry Lehman, Steve Phillips, Lou Ann Smith, Mark Winstanley, R. J. Marx, staff of the *Seaside Signal*, staff of the Chamber of Commerce, staff of the visitors bureau, the Seaside Downtown Development Association, and Melissa Ousley, my editor.

Table of Contents

CHAPTER 1

1941

―――――

MEMORIAL DAY WEEKEND, 1941

THE TOWN SLOWLY STIRRED FROM a long winter's nap. It would have been nice to stay asleep just a tad longer. It was time to wake and get ready for the new adventure. Activity was starting.

Merchants cleaned their shops that had been closed all winter. Windows were washed and gleamed in the sunshine. Stores were being swept, floors mopped, and new merchandise brought in. Soon the main street would be lively with tourists and summer residents.

People were opening motel rooms and summer homes. After a long, dark, damp winter, homes and rooms needed to be aired out—fresh air in, cold, damp air out. Dusting and sweeping were the order of the day. Washed and starched curtains hung over spotless windows. The furniture was polished and dusted. The smell of polish and bleach filled the air. Everything had to be cleaned and shined.

City workers were busy putting up the lifeguard stand, just in front of the turnaround, with the smaller stands spaced several blocks apart on the beach. This was one of the main attractions of this summer tourist town. The beach, with its grassy dunes, was long and wide. The blue Pacific Ocean was not always gentle on this part of Oregon's coast. The ocean was filled with hidden dangers—large crab holes, rip tides, and strong currents. The lifeguards were essential to the safety of residents and tourists.

The Prom, a concrete path running the length of the beach, was the place where many tourists would be found. It was custom to take walks in the long summer evenings and to sit on the benches, while spectacular and colorful sunsets filled the sky.

During the day, the beach would be crowded with young people soaking up the sun and getting tan. The smell of cocoa butter, mixed with baby oil—a sure recipe for a summer tan—would fill the air. It mixed with the aromas of popcorn, caramel corn, hot dogs, and saltwater taffy.

Built on the Prom and fronting the ocean was the indoor natatorium. It housed three large, heated saltwater pools for swimming, plus two diving boards. It was believed the heated salt water was good for health. After a swim, a sauna room with wooden benches could be used for relaxing. It was a perfect way to unwind after a few hours of exercise. The room would fill with steam, which would mix with the strong scent of wet bathing suits and salt water.

Next to the natatorium was the Prom Bicycle Shop. All types of bikes could be rented—single bikes, small and large ones, or tricycles. The most popular were the tandem bikes; they enabled best friends to ride together. The Prom was the ideal place to ride: it was approximately one and a half miles long and fairly easy to complete, taking only an hour of rental time.

One of the most visited spots was the aquarium, situated just a short walk north on the Prom from Broadway. The aquarium, a large wooden building, housed a seal tank at the front to draw people in. At the admission desk, a person could buy food for these ocean performers—oh, how the seals loved their fish! Each seal had a name and could perform a different trick to attract the attention of the patrons. They splashed water with their flippers and barked loudly if people overlooked them or did not feed them fast enough. They were such cute performers, whom no one could resist. They were fed well by the curator of the aquarium, but they certainly loved to show off for the visitors.

Along the sides of the large, dark, round room behind the seals were many tanks brimming with different types of sea creatures, making people feel as if they were actually underwater. A large octopus in the center of the room would crawl lazily around its tank. It was up close and personal, allowing viewers to see its long, skinny tentacles covered with suction cups.

The tank with sea anemones was filled with all the colors of the rainbow. These beautiful creatures, when they gently swayed back and forth, seemed to do ballet to unheard music. They were extremely graceful and a joy to watch. The young people loved the aquarium and would spend many hours watching everything that happened. Perhaps some of them went on to study marine biology.

Broadway was the main street in this small coastal city, a street where people could buy everything they needed to complete a perfect day at the beach. T-shirts, sweatshirts, flip-flops, hats, sunscreen, and sunglasses were readily available for purchase.

One of the most exciting attractions was the merry-go-round. The sound of the calliope music could be heard blocks away and always attracted visitors to its site. The price was right, only a nickel, and if visitors were lucky, they could catch the brass ring and enjoy a free ride. This was one of the original structures, and all of the animals were made of wood. The horses were brightly painted and were so proud looking while they went round and round.

In the 1990s, the merry-go-round was taken to the carousel museum in Portland and featured as one of the oldest rides. It was restored and preserved for future generations to admire. A new one was put in its place, comprising horses and other animals made of Plexiglas.

They are still brightly painted, and the calliope music can still be heard on the street, to the delight of the tourists.

A tilt-a-whirl and miniature bowling completed the amusements center. Across the street was a Ferris wheel. The operator always stopped the wheel when people were right on top. The view was terrific from this vantage, but the height would become terrifying if an occupant's partner rocked the car. Screams of delight were often heard from the participants enjoying the rides.

The town had two movie houses, both owned by the same individual. The older one showed B films and old westerns. The new theater showed first-rate films—the best and latest in Hollywood. On Saturday afternoons, the children would fill the old theater to watch serials, such as *The Lone Ranger*, *The Cisco Kid*, and *Flash Gordon*. Each youngster would vow to come back the following week to see the next installment. Could any of the exciting machines shown in the Flash Gordon movies come to exist in their future? The children would hotly debate this question after leaving the movie house.

A twelve-lane bowling alley on the main street was a well-respected hangout. League bowling was a big sport in the 1940s. In the winter months, most of the local residents would enjoy an evening competition for the championship. Open bowling filled the summer months with packed lanes. After watching for a while, a spectator would cease to notice the constant noise of balls being hurled down the alleys and their returning to the racks. The rhythm of the pinsetters was mesmerizing, as was their quickness and accuracy. The job was a good one for the young men of the town.

The roller-skating rink was a popular place. The choreographed skating with intricate steps, timed with the pulsating sound of organ music, was a treat to watch. The girls wore short, full skirts, as well as matching tassels on their white skates. The boys wore slacks with matching shirts and black skates. Only the best skaters took the center of the rink and performed the various dance routines. After a number, the audience would applaud to show their appreciation for a fine performance. Other skaters, those with limited abilities, could only look on with awe. By constantly practicing, perhaps they would be ready to take the center of the rink some day and bask in the adoration of the audience.

By far, the most wonderful place was the Bungalow Dance Hall, an old wooden building that had crepe paper streamers hanging lazily from its ceiling and a large stage for an orchestra. Drinking and smoking were not allowed, making it a perfectly safe place for all. Young ladies could go alone or with a girlfriend. Many young men often went stag—that is, they attended without a date. It was not uncommon for people to dance the entire evening with others they had not previously met. Sometimes a big band, one that everyone had heard of, would arrive in town, and the dance hall would fill to capacity. Different parts of the country had various styles of dancing. The young ladies could always follow, if they found a good partner. Every Saturday evening, the young people gathered and jitterbugged the evening away. All bands had a very attractive female singer who would dress in a long evening gown. When she took center stage to create a rendition of a popular song, it was customary to gather around the bandstand to listen intently. Good manners always prevailed.

Each Saturday afternoon, the Seaside Girls Band assembled at the old grade school to march on Broadway. The uniforms consisted of blue skirts, white blouses, and blue capes. On the left arm, the cape was thrown over the shoulder so that the gold lining showed. The band only played Sousa marches and patriotic songs. The band proudly boasted a majorette, dressed in a shiny-white-satin uniform and boots. She would toss her silver baton high in the air, turn around in a circle, and catch it on the way down, always to the applause of the visitors. At times there was an occasional sour note—someone would be out of step, but the people who lined Broadway didn't seem to mind.

At the start of the summer season, the pony lady would arrive. Nobody really knew her name. She had gray hair tied back into a bun, situated underneath a floppy hat, and she wore a wide skirt, cowboy shirt, and boots. She drove a string of four or five Shetland ponies and set her shelter on the beach, just north of the Turnaround. For a nickel, a young child could ride a pony to Twelfth Avenue and back. It was quite an attraction and always had a line of youngsters eagerly waiting for a ride.

The town had a fine volunteer fire department, consisting mostly of businessmen. When the siren blew, townspeople would see many men leave their stores to answer the call. There were two fire trucks, which was more than adequate to serve the town.

The police department was manned by the chief and two officers. They were kept quite busy during the summer months. There were no major crimes in the city, mostly lost children and a few rowdy teenagers. The jail was located on the ground floor of city hall and had three holding cells.

Now everyone was ready for the summer to start. The stores were well stocked with new merchandise. Summer help had been hired and trained, ready to assist all customers. It was Memorial Day weekend of 1941, and the town opened up to welcome all the tourists and summer folks.

Past the commercial part of town, everything was different. There, great beauty could be found. Two rivers bisected the town. The Necanicum ran through the heart of the town. There were several bridges across the river, so people could go from east to west. By far, the Broadway Bridge was the most intriguing: composed of concrete with beautiful designs, it expressed sturdiness and durability. The other bridges were wooden, and the planks were spaced a little apart; when crossing, people could look down at the water.

On the west, the town faced the Pacific Ocean. The beauty and strength of this magnificent body of water inspired awe and adventure. Residents who grew up in Seaside had a healthy respect for the water. Very few people swam alone, always with a buddy. The other three sides of the town were surrounded by green forests. To a small child, some of the trees looked like they touched the sky. Gigantic, white, fluffy clouds sometimes filled the sky. There was nothing more beautiful and pleasant than lying on the riverbank while looking up at a brilliant-blue sky ringed with billowing clouds.

The second river, the Neawanna, was toward the eastern part of the city. This smaller body of water had only a few people living nearby. Farms bordered this section of town. Here, people could buy fresh eggs and, during the summer, fresh berries. Agriculture was not a big part of the town, but for the people who lived in this area, it was a very good business. This was a lovely spot to take a nature walk. Birds would sing, and small critters would scamper around. Occasionally, deer and elk were spotted. It was so quiet there: a person could almost forget that a commercial area was close.

On the banks of the Necanicum, the loggers held their annual picnic toward the last part of summer. This was a fantastic event—teeming with axe throwing, climbing of the greased pole, log sawing, and log rolling. The fastest individual in each sport was declared the winner. Great times were had by all. Of course, after each event the winner was treated to a free beer, so sometimes things got a little bit out of hand. In general, however, everyone looked forward to this event. It was good, clean fun and gave the hardworking loggers a chance to show off their talents. These were the men who kept the town's industry running, which provided good jobs for many of the citizens.

There was another part of the town. In 1805, when the Lewis and Clark expedition were wintering over at Fort Clatsop, five men were dispensed to the beach to extract salt from the seawater. They performed this task at the beach in Seaside. They boiled salt water in kettles over an open fire. As the water boiled down, they extracted pure, white salt, which was then strained and dried. After a little over two months, they had three and a half bushels of salt, approximately 175 pounds. This was used to preserve their meat at the fort. In 1903, Jenny Michel, a Clatsop Native American, showed the residents of the town where her mother had informed her she had seen white men boiling water. The salt works is preserved in the town as one of the historical sites.

Jenny Michel lived until 1903 and was known for her beautiful weaving. Her baskets and mats were greatly desired. She sold many of her works to full-time residents and tourists. It was always an honor to meet her and purchase one of her intricate, beautiful works of art. Some of her baskets are displayed at the Smithsonian Institute.

South of town, at the cove, there was a gravesite marked "Known Only to God." These buried individuals were found on the beach on April 24, 1865. The story behind this site describes a small sailing vessel that was anchored in the ocean. Three men rowed in to find fresh water. They met some citizens of the town, who assisted them with their task. After filling their buckets, they started back to the ship. However, a storm came quickly, catching them between the shore and the ship. The men of Seaside built a bonfire on the beach to show them the way back to shore. The next morning, the sailing ship was gone, and three bodies had washed up on the shore. The residents buried the men on the beach. Their nationality remains unknown, as well as the name of the sailing vessel. One can only imagine the sorrow of the wives and mothers upon the ship's docking, when they realized their loved ones were not among the remaining crew. No one on the vessel was fully aware of the citizens' loving and caring disposition. Today, the grave is maintained by the local residents who live nearby. It is one of the many historical landmarks in the town.

Little did the town or the people know this would be the last summer for innocence and fun. Doors to the homes were never locked. After completing their chores around the house, young kids take off to play. There was always the beach to explore, a place where new shells could always be found. If a person was lucky, he or she would find a glass float among the sea grass. Hide-and-seek was one of the more popular games played. A baseball and bat could entertain a group of young people for hours. There were few worries for the young citizens of this town. People were very friendly and always willing to assist someone in need. When the mothers called for dinnertime, games were stopped immediately, and everyone went home. At the dining table, the talk was about the day's activities. After dinner, it was a marvelous time to take a stroll on the Prom and watch the sunset.

The world on both sides of the United States was filled with hate, anger, and war. Japan was leaving destruction and death in its conquest of China. In Europe, Germany was marching into every county. England was undergoing constant bombardment every night; its cities were being destroyed, and its lives were being lost.

The United States kept out of the war, but many wondered for how long it could remain detached. Many of the young men in the Air Force were giving up their commissions to go to China to join the Chinese Air Force. This was the first American Volunteer Group, commanded by Claire L. Chennault, a retired US Army Air Corps officer who had worked in China since 1937. He was also a military advisor to Generalissimo Chiang Kai-shek. Since the United States was not at war, this special air unit could not operate openly, but at the request of President Roosevelt, it was approved. The AVG group was known as the Flying Tigers, due to the distinctive marking of the nose of the planes.

During the summer and fall of 1941, over three hundred men sailed for Burma. This included ninety-nine pilots and two hundred ground crewmen. Also shipped on the boat were one hundred P-40s planes. A schoolhouse was set up for training and operations. Chennault had a different tactic for air battles, based on his observation of the Japanese pilots. Some men washed out immediately, and others quit at the first opportunity. The Flying Tigers was comprised of sixty-two trained combat and fighter pilots. The men wore a particular patch on the backs of their jackets. The patch was a replica of the Chinese flag and had lettering that read, "This foreign person has come to China to help in the war effort. Soldiers and civilians, one and all, should rescue and protect him." (R. E. Baldwin Collection) The Flying Tigers existed until the end of 1942. This elite group of men was later honored for their bravery and courage.

Other young pilots went to England to fight in the British Royal Air Force. These men were welcomed because England was trying desperately to prevail in its fight with the German air force. Some British parents were sending their children to America to keep them safe. Most people felt that President Roosevelt would keep the county out of the war. He had pulled the United States out of the Great Depression when he took office in 1932. To be brought into this war was too horrific for most Americans to contemplate. This ubiquitous feeling was the main reason why the town found worldwide events concerning the war to be extremely important.

The summer of 1941 was a time for playing on the beach, for dancing the night away, and for just having fun. It was a glorious summer that year. Without television, computers, and mobile phones, war news slowly reached the general public. The most recent news would be shown in the newsreels at the movies, usually about two weeks later.

Summer passed all too quickly for the tourists and summer residents. It was now time for one last weekend—Labor Day. This always signaled the end of the summer season. On the Monday ending the weekend, an individual could walk down Seaside's main street and not see a car or person. The tourists and summer residents returned to their homes in Portland, elsewhere preparing for the school year to start.

Most of the shops along Broadway closed up for the winter. After shop owners thoroughly cleaned their stores and put away summer merchandise that had not sold, they boarded up their windows. Doing so provided protection from the fierce winter storms; pouring rain and blustery winds could be a problem for a building left unattended.

The business's that stayed open all winter sold the basic necessities to the townspeople. Piggly Wiggly was the main food store, and the town had two or three other mom-and-pop groceries stores. Wheatley's Dry Goods and Seaside Hardware sold mostly everything a person might need to get through winter. Seaside Signal Oil was ready to service all furnaces or fill tanks with fuel for the cold rainy months ahead. It was also necessary to purchase wood for fireplaces, or an individual could go into the woods and chop their own. The warm, soothing glow always made home special. The aroma of wood burning was pleasing and the crackling of fires made everything feel cozy and safe. The war seemed a long way off; many likely believed it wouldn't come to affect them.

Then, after the summer's closing, the town belonged to the local residents. In comparison with today's society, the entertainment might seem boring and laughable. Every home had a radio. The sounds of Bob Hope, Burns and Allen, Lux Radio Show, The Shadows Knows, Boston Blackie, and many more filled the living rooms. Some of the shows were so scary that when youngsters went to bed, they would cover their heads with blankets and hope the monsters would stay away.

When fall arrived, the days and evening became a little bit cooler, signaling the time to bring out those sweaters and jackets. The leaves on the trees turned into brilliant fall colors of flaming reds, bright yellows, and shocking oranges. The season brought much beauty to the town.

The high school football games took place every Friday. When the games were played out of town, people filled up their cars with neighbors and made the trip to other communities. All basketball games were held in the gymnasium, and the stands were jam-packed with local residents cheering on their team. For out-of-town games, people carpooled and went to neighboring cities to cheer their team.

Every Wednesday evening, the town sponsored a community sing that was held in the auditorium of the grade school. The judge of Seaside, who had a robust voice, led the singing, and his wife played the piano. Around one to two hundred people attended these sing-a-longs, and great fun was had by all. A community sing was a wonderful way to spend a winter's evening.

Three times a year, the Seaside Girls Band put on a concert, fall, spring, and winter. The music was suited to each season. These concerts were always appreciated by the audiences (especially the mothers and fathers of the musicians) and gave the young people a sense of purpose and direction.

The new movie theater, The Times, had the very latest films from Hollywood. Teenage girls would swoon over John Wayne, Errol Flynn, Tyrone Power, Alan Ladd, Ronald Reagan, and other film hero's. The young men enjoyed watching Lana Turner, Betty Grable, Esther Williams, and Rita Hayworth. Would they ever meet a lady as beautiful and talented as these film stars were? Probably not in

Seaside, but it was interesting to daydream about all the adventures shown on the films. This was the day of musicals, with the thrilling voice of Jane Powell, a former resident of Portland, Deane Durbin, Gloria Jean, and Judy Garland. Elaborate tap-dance numbers were staged and starred Fred Astaire, Gene Kelly, Debbie Reynolds, and Ann Miller. Movies were always appropriate for all ages.

October was time for Halloween and trick-or-treating. Mostly it was just treating, and the tricks played were harmless and good-natured fun. One Halloween was especially memorable. It was the year that Orson Wells appeared on the radio with *War of the Worlds*. During the breaks, it was announced this was just a play. Due to the genius of Mr. Wells and the production, the reaction of most of the general public was horrifying. Many parents held their children tightly, feeling as if the world were coming to an end. After they sensed that it was just a radio show and not real life, things returned to normal.

Thanksgiving was almost here. Mothers were busy cooking pies, making stuffing for the turkey, and baking homemade rolls. In those days, everything was prepared by hand. The bouquets of all the spices mixed together were exotic. Kids ran to the kitchen to ask when dinner would be ready. Finally, the family and all the guests sat down at the table together. Father said grace, and each person told what he or she was thankful for. After a large, delicious meal, what could be better than settling down and listening to the football game on the radio or, if the weather permitted, walking on the Prom to settle all that food. Mother and the girls did dishes. There were so many, but no one seemed to mind. The meal had been scrumptious, one that the family would be talking about for a week.

The days were growing shorter and darker as winter settled in. During these long, dark, rainy days, home became quite welcoming. A nice fire crackling, food cooking on the stove, the paper waiting to be read—this was heaven. It was a simple lifestyle, where pleasures centered on the home and family.

The residents were getting their thoughts in order to celebrate Christmas season. Stores decorated their windows with Santa Clauses and manger sets. Almost all decorating for Christmas was done the day after Thanksgiving. Children were excited and counted the days until the big event arrived. Even the rain and winter storms could not dampen their spirits. Cards had to be purchased and sent to friends and relatives near and far. Tasteful wrapping paper and colored ribbons filled spare rooms. Gifts were hidden away from the prying eyes of snooping young children. Letters were written to Santa Clause and quickly mailed, each one filled with wishes for a magnificent Christmas Day. Choirs of the local churches were busily practicing their music, so when the day arrived the town would be filled with the glorious sound of carols.

December started off as all of the other winter months had. The Japanese diplomats were in Washington, DC, holding conferences with President Roosevelt. It seemed these were going quite well. Perhaps we would be kept out of the war, or maybe peace would be negotiated.

At the coast, the weather was cold and damp. On Sunday, December 7, most of the town's residents were in their houses of worship. Suddenly, the fire siren sounded but in a different tone. It was one long, high-pitched sound that seemed to go on forever.

Worship services were halted. Clergymen, in hushed tones, gave the congregations the news. Japanese airplanes had bombed Pearl Harbor, Hawaii. There were many casualties. Most of the Naval Fleet had been destroyed or seriously damaged. A prayer for peace was given, and then everyone was dismissed. At home, people huddled around their radios, listening intently for the latest news. How could this happen? Why were we not prepared to defend ourselves? What would happen next? Were the Japanese already heading to the coast to do more damage? So many thoughts were running through everyone's mind.

The day passed rapidly. By evening, everyone in this coastal town had been told to have no lights showing. If townspeople drove at night, they placed cloth or newspaper over their headlights. Houses were dark; no streetlights were on. No one left their radios. Everyone listened for the latest news. Finally, casualty numbers came in. Over two thousand of our young men had been killed. Many more were wounded. Our fleet had been nearly eliminated. What was next? The West Coast felt defenseless.

The next day, every recruiting station had lines around the block. Young, middle-aged, and old men were anxious to join the military. Some of the young men lied about their ages, but they were soon discovered and sent home to wait until they had reached the age of eighteen.

At school on Monday, all the pupils were gathered in the auditorium. President Roosevelt was to make a speech, to declare war against Japan, Germany, and Italy. It was a day that no one would forget. The siren started up again, and school was dismissed. It was believed that the Japanese had launched an air attack on the United States. Students scrambled to get schoolbooks and ran to the safety of their homes. The world had changed overnight. Gone was all the excitement over the coming of Christmas. The only thoughts on people's minds were war and how to prepare.

Meetings were held in town to decide how to proceed with rules and regulations. The Army announced that no one would be allowed on the beach or the Prom after 4:30 p.m. in the winter. Summer curfew would be 8:30 p.m. Many of the town's men volunteered to become air raid wardens. Schedules were developed and followed closely. Various sites were selected to watch for enemy planes. One site was on top of the Times Theater. The Army quickly built a gun station on Tillamook Head. It was manned by soldiers. Men patrolled the city to ensure that lights were not showing from houses. If people had painted white rocks in their yards, they were instructed to flip the rocks over. Air raid shelters were designated throughout the town. Residents were instructed to go to the nearest safe accommodations in the event of an emergency.

Wheatley's Dry Goods sold out of the materials used to sew blackout curtains, which could hide the lights in the evening. School officials were instructed on safety procedures in the event of an air raid. The grade school had an underground facility that was used for the cafeteria; all students were instructed to go there immediately if an air raid occurred. The high school students were to go to the bottom floor of the school. Food and gas were rationed. Automobile plants switched to producing jeeps and other vehicles for the armed forces. It was now impossible for people to purchase new automobiles or even new tires for their cars.

Each family was issued rationing books filled with coupons for purchasing supplies and food. The number of stamps was dependent upon the size of the family. Sugar, flour, coffee, cigarettes, and shoes were some of the items that were hard to find. The black market sprung up with unscrupulous individuals peddling scare items for a profit. These occurred mostly in large cities. Most citizens would not support them because to do so was considered extremely unpatriotic. If a family had an emergency, they could always trade stamps with another family to meet their needs.

The casualty count from the attack on Pearl Harbor was finally ascertained: over two thousand men had been killed in a few hours. The Navy made the decision not to raise the USS *Arizona*, but to let her lie at the bottom of the harbor with all the personnel left where they had been killed. Other battleships and destroyers were repaired as thoroughly as possible.

The Japanese Army could not be stopped at the beginning of the war. They invaded the Philippines, and many of our men were captured, along with Army and Navy nurses. The men were marched to Bataan, under extreme circumstances of hunger and thirst. This became known as the Bataan Death March.

Some of the residents of the town had relatives in the Philippines, and they were very worried. Were they all right? How would they survive in the concentration camps?

The Army and Navy nurses were sent to Santo Tomas Internment Camp. In May 1943, the Navy nurses were transferred to Los Banos.

Santo Tomas had been the university, and the dormitories held all of the civilians who were unable to escape. Many were families of servicemen stationed in the Philippines. Most didn't know whether their husbands were alive or had been killed in the first few days of the fighting. The closeness of other families was very comforting to all who were held in this prison camp.

Captain Maude C. Davison, with twenty years of service experience, was in command of the nurses. She maintained a regular schedule of nursing duty and was adamant that all nurses should wear their khaki blouses and skirts while on duty. This gave a sense of order to their days and assisted in giving them purpose while being held prisoners.

The Navy nurses were under the command of Lt. Cobb. After their transfer to Los Banos, they established a new infirmary and continued working as a nursing unit. There they were known as the "Sacred Eleven."

During their final year of internment, January 1944, control of the Santo Tomas camp shifted from Japanese civil authorities to the Imperial Japanese Army. This caused more difficulties for the prisoners. Access to outside food services was curtailed, and the diet of the internees was reduced to 900 calories per person per day. In January 1945, it was further reduced to 700 calories per day. The nurses, on average, lost approximately 30 percent of their individual body weight. They also experienced a degree of service-connected disability, the same as the male POWs.

As these pieces of news were reported at home, people became incensed at the brutality of the Japanese army. People watched hopelessly while Guam, Wake, and Iwo Jima fell to the advancing enemy army.

On February 3, 1945, the US Army liberated the Philippine islands. Santo Tomas Internment Camp was one of the first places that greeted the Army. After civilians and nurses received first aid and food, arrangements were made to send all civilians to Honolulu and then home to the United States. The Navy nurses were liberated by the US Army at Los Banos a few days later. Upon returning to the United States, the US Army nurses were awarded the Bronze Star for valor and a Presidential Unit Citation for extraordinary heroism in action. The Navy nurses were also awarded the Bronze Star for their heroic actions.

In Seaside there was a Japanese American family who owned a small curio store on Broadway. It was a favorite shop of the youngsters. For a nickel, a kid could purchase a small shell; when placed in water, these shells would open and reveal a paper flower. They were extremely friendly, a delightful family consisting of a daughter and son. No one in the town thought differently about them after Pearl Harbor.

The country was in mass hysteria about the large number of Japanese living on the coast. On February 19, 1942, President Roosevelt signed Executive Order 9066, an executive law that would displace 122,000 Japanese people from the coast, including 70,000 Japanese American citizens. They were placed in internment camps further inland. The family from Seaside sold its business and was sent to one of these camps.

The internment camps were called resettlement centers but were more like penitentiaries, with armed guards in towers with spotlights and deadly tommy guns, fifteen feet of barbed fences. Everyone was confined to quarters at 9:00 p.m., with lights out at 10:00 p.m. No one was allowed to take the two-block-long hike to the latrines after nine, under any circumstances.

Food and sanitation were the worst. There was no fresh meat, vegetables, or butter. Eventually, when it became possible, vegetable gardens were planted and harvested. Many people in Seaside worried about the Japanese family. Would they ever be able to return to the town and reestablish their business? They did not return to Seaside after the war.

Many of the young men, who were relocated, joined the US Army. The total number was thirty thousand Japanese Americans men who served in the US Army, in segregated units. They served with distinction and many were cited for bravery. The irony of the situation was not lost on these soldiers. While they were fighting for their country, their families were still held in the relocation camps.

Christmas had arrived, and although people celebrated the birth of The Lord, it was a very different season. Many of the young men had left the area to join branches of the service. Everyone tried to keep up a good presence; it was evident there was a great deal of worry. The churches held their midnight services, the choir sang hymns and carols, and people prayed for peace.

In the homes, people decorated their trees, opened presents, and tried to have a good Christmas dinner. Meat was getting harder to find, but meatless meals were becoming commonplace and people managed. As soon as the weather permitted, victory gardens were planted. If people couldn't have meat for every dinner, at least they could have fresh vegetables. On the coast, razor clams and crabs were available.

January was the hardest month. It got dark at 4:30 p.m., and the lack of streetlights and home lights cast gloom on the town. The residents took a while to adjust to the constant darkness. The only amusement was the movies. Hollywood was turning out war films, most of them propaganda about the enemies. There were some excellent movies, such as *Mrs. Miniver*. It introduced audiences to Greer Garson, who went on to become a very popular star.

The radio became the source of news. Every evening, the people gathered around and listened to the very latest situation. The moves always had a newsreel before the main feature. Pictures of the war were about two weeks behind, but at least they gave descriptions of what was going on. There were two major newspapers in Portland, *The Oregonian* and *The Journal*. Both of these excellent papers gave accurate news on the war. Weekly magazines, such as *Life*, *Time*, and *The Saturday Evening Post*, gave in-depth stories about the war effort.

The war greatly affected the women on the home front. Most of the men were in the armed services. The airplane factories and other defense plants desperately needed workers. Rosie the Riveter was now in style. The townspeople saw her poster everywhere, a woman in coveralls, hair tied in a bandana on her head, flexing her muscle. She was doing her part to help the war effort. "What were you doing" was the message. Most women had never worked outside of their homes, so there was a challenge. Women joined the workforce by the thousands. They did all kinds of work that was extremely important to the war effort.

This had an impact on Seaside. Suddenly, women were gone from the home. There were no defense plants in the town; however, there was other work that needed to be done. Businesses needed clerks, and offices needed help to run their establishments. The Red Cross headquarters sometimes sent out calls for help. Women rolled bandages that would be sent to the various military bases. Lonely young men, away from the home for the first time, very often needed assistance. There were letter writing to their homes, worries about families, and wives who were left with small children. The volunteers offered a sympathetic ear and help whenever they could. Many of the young men just needed someone to talk to. Telephone calls to homes were very important to these boys and could be made at the Red Cross. The coffee pot was always filled, and donuts were available.

In Astoria, the fishing industry was suddenly hit with a shortage of workers. At that time, there were over fifty canneries on the river. The Daughters of the Columbia rallied to the call. Women operated fishing boats, while their husbands were off fighting the war. Once again, women took over. They ran the bars, restaurants, and shops, making considerable contributions to the war effort. Tongue Point Naval Air Station was a training place for many pilots. Astoria, which had been a small fishing village on the Columbia River, became a very important factor in the war effort.

One of the biggest challenges came with women joining the military. In September 1942, the Women's Auxiliary Ferry Squadron was created. It included twenty-eight women who had at least 800 hours flying time and a 200-horsepower rating. The squadron's original mission was to ferry Army Air Force trainers and light aircraft from the factories to the military bases, but later on they delivered fighters and bombers and provided transport as well. Eventually the squadron had 1,074 pilots, each one freeing up a male pilot for combat missions. The squadron was under the leadership of Nancy Harkness Love.

Other branches of military service opened up to women. The Army, Navy, Marine Corps, and Coast Guard all recruited women. Nurses were especially needed to assist with the wounded. All women who served were invaluable to the war effort.

The grade school and high school students in Seaside also volunteered. Paper, aluminum, and scrap-metal drives were held. Once collected, such material was then shipped to wherever it was needed. This gave the young people a sense that they, too, were aiding the war effort.

Another important work was helping the vegetable and fruit growers pick their crops. Just north of Seaside were cranberry bogs, and before Thanksgiving they needed harvesting. Today, the cranberry bogs are flooded with water before the berries are gathered by machines. Not so in the 1940s. Sometimes pupils would be dismissed from school for a day and transported to Warrenton to pick these berries. Most of the young people volunteered, and off they would go on school buses to do their part for the war. Not too many of the students knew how to do this job or how hard it could be. To harvest the berries, they got on their hands and knees and picked through the thick bushes, even when it was cold and raining. After lunch breaks, most wanted to go back to school or at least sit in the warm bus. They stuck it out until 3:00 p.m. The pay was five cents a basket, and most didn't make more than twenty cents in a days' work. However, it was all for the war effort, so our troops would have cranberry sauce with their Thanksgiving dinner.

War bonds were sold everywhere. For an investment of $18.75, held for 10 years, a person would receive $25.00 from the government. In order to sell more, the government offered stamps for twenty-five cents, which were then pasted in a bond book. When an individual had acquired $18.75, he or she received a war bond. Young people saved their nickels and dimes to aid in the fight for freedom. At many dances held at Seaside's high school, the young lady who had sold the most war bonds was honored as bond queen.

In Astoria, the county seat, the United Service Organization (USO) was established. It was a home away from home for many of the young men in the service. Dances were held every weekend. Almost all of the young girls volunteered to attend. Seaside's young ladies were transported by school buses to Astoria, along with chaperones. The rules were strict: girls had to dance with any young servicemen who asked them. However, the girls were only allowed to dance three times with the same person. It was permissible for a girl to give her first name to her dance partner—but no last name, no phone number, and no personal information. However, if a girl wanted to see a young man, there were always ways to get around the rules and not be caught. Girls, perhaps, could let it slip where they worked and what shift they had. Romance was always blooming.

The majority of these young men were far from their homes, so they deeply appreciated all of the hospitality shown to them. It was common for townspeople's homes to have at least two or three servicemen at Sunday dinner. These men were so young and frightened. What would happen after they left the United States? Would they ever see their families or homes again? The time spent with the residents of the town gave comfort to many of these servicemen.

Many of the young men were from the Midwest. The ocean was such a novelty to them. Their reaction was always one of amazement at the power and beauty of the majestic waves. Pictures were taken with the ocean in the background. The families at home would have a souvenir of their days in Seaside.

The winter was slowly giving up its long hold on the town, and spring was arriving. The days were becoming longer and slightly warmer. With all the variety of flowers blooming, color was creeping back into the town. The merchants wondered what kind of summer they would have. It was doubtful whether many of the tourists could spend their precious gas coupons to come to town for a day. They knew the summer residents, wives, and families would be here, and the fathers would arrive on the train Friday evenings and leave Sunday afternoons.

There were new families coming in, and they rented almost every space in town. These were the families of the servicemen who were stationed at Camp Rilea, Fort Stevens, and Tongue Point. What a wonderful addition to the town. Schools suddenly had an influx of young people. Now when going into town, townspeople could hear different accents and meet people from many diverse sections of the country. It was an enjoyable experience.

Memorial Day 1942 arrived, and once again the town opened up to as many visitors as could come. The lifeguard stands were erected on the beach. All of the stores opened on Broadway, but with a few differences.

One of the oldest businesses on the coast is Phillips Candy Store, founded in 1897 by the Riggsby Brothers of Astoria and originally opened as a cigar and candy store. Mr. and Mrs. Phillips purchased the store in 1939. It has been in the family ever since, currently run by Steve Phillips, the youngest son. Each day, fresh saltwater taffy is made and put in the bins. There is a wrapping machine for the taffy in the store that dates back to the 1940s. All types of candy can be purchased, and always the freshest in town.

Due to the rationing of sugar, the store was limited in how much candy it could produce. People lined up outside of its door around noon each day. At 1:00 p.m., the store opened for business. Each customer was limited to one pound of candy. A family of four could buy four pounds. When all the candy had been sold, usually around 2:30 p.m., the store closed its doors. Many of the other shops were short on merchandise, but all managed to sell what they had.

June arrived with its usual burst of color. By now, people were slowly getting used to all of the rationing and the 8:30 p.m. curfew for the beach. A nice stroll down Broadway was a lovely way to spend summer evenings.

On the evening of June 21, 1942, the war reached Seaside. One family who lived on the Prom reported the incident as follows: Their two daughters were having a slumber party. As the lights were off, the family had the blackout curtain open. Around 10:30 p.m., suddenly there were loud noises—sounding like cannon fire—and flashes of light coming from the ocean. The daughters, with their friends, ran out on the Prom to see what was going on. The Military Police came by in their jeep and told the girls to go back inside—a Japanese submarine had penetrated security and was shelling the coast of Oregon. The girls were fascinated and stood on the Prom, watching the event.

After about ten minutes, the dad came out of the house and ordered the girls back into safety. Years later, one of them remarked that it probably wasn't the best idea they had ever had—the Japanese could have been landing troops in front of their home. However, that was not their thought at the time of the attack, just that they were witnessing history. The object of the sub's attack was to inflict damage on the mouth of the Columbia River and to knock out Fort Steven's guns.

The Columbia River was very important to the war effort. Kaiser was building liberty ships in Portland, and they were traveling down the river to head overseas. Damage to the river could have delayed our preparedness. However, the sub was approximately eight miles south of its intended target, shelling a deserted beach. Even today, many stories abound as to why the fort did not open fire. It had the sub in range and could have destroyed it. The Officer in Charge of the fort gave the order that no one was to fire, because they did not want the sub to realize how far off course they were. It was very difficult for the men to hold back, but cooler heads prevailed—no guns were fired. A few shells landed in Warrenton, and there is a monument placed there. Fort Stevens had many souvenirs of the shelling. For the first time since the building of Tillamook Rock Light House, the beacon was turned off. The information about the shelling was not readily given to the newspapers around the country; the government did not want the public to know how unprepared and how weak our defenses had been.

It was a wake-up call for the town—it realized how easily the Japanese could have launched an invasion. Following the attack, all rules and regulations concerning the war and our defenses were vigorously obeyed. Doing so had a very sobering effect on the town.

The amount of servicemen doubled at the various bases, and Seaside overflowed as a result. The Bungalow Dance Hall was now filled at every dance. The USO was operating to full capacity. All the ladies at the Red Cross Center doubled their efforts in rolling bandages and being of assistance to the young servicemen.

Still the war news was not good. It seemed like nothing could stop the enemy from advancing to wherever they desired. More and more of the young servicemen were being deployed to fight overseas. Would it ever turn around? At the home front, many families were changing their window displays from a star, which indicated a loved one being in the service, to a gold star, which indicated a death of a young man or woman.

The proprietors of Leonard's Salt Water Taffy Shop lived in Portland during the winter months. They stayed in town during the summer to run their shop. Suddenly a gold star was placed in their window, indicating their only son had been killed overseas. This was the only Seaside resident killed in action.

Many of the sons of the townspeople had harrowing experiences during the war years. One family, the Norelius, cousins to the author, had one son in the Air Force who was shot down over occupied France, and he was held in a prisoner-of-war camp. He and a fellow prisoner, an Englishman, planned and executed a successful escape. The French partisans assisted them. They were given civilian clothes and were informed of safe houses along the way to Allied lines. At one point they rested in a barn up in a hayloft. The kindly farmers provided them with a loaf of bread and a bottle of wine. While relaxing in the loft, suddenly they heard the barn door open. Just below them entered a small German unit, seeking shelter from the rain. The men were paralyzed with fear. Exposure would mean instant death to them and the farmer and his family. This horrendous situation continued for about one hour, until the Germans left. To the men hiding, it seemed like an eternity.

Nick Norelius suffered from frostbite as he forged rivers and streams to borrow rowboats. They finally reached friendly lines, and

each was returned to his unit. Once back home, Norelius was pre-
sented with a boot emblem with wings to symbolize his escape. This
was worn under the lapel of his uniform. He could no longer fly
over Europe, and spent the rest of his enlistment in the United States
teaching survival methods to pilots.

After his discharge from the Air Force, he entered college under
the GI Bill and became an engineer. He never talked about his escape
again, only when he first came home. The family respected his pri-
vacy; no questions were ever asked.

His younger brother, Richard, was in the Navy and had three
ships shot out from under him. He had seen many of his shipmates
perish and was in a troubled state of mind. Both were granted leave at
the same time and returned to Seaside for a thirty-day rest. The entire
town welcomed them, treating them as the hero's they were. They had
free meals at the various restaurants, courtesy of local residents. Also,
they were given free passes to the movie theater. With the love of their
family and friends, both recovered in Seaside. The town felt blessed
that they had returned safely, even it if were for only thirty days.

However, the younger brother had difficulty readjusting to civilian life after his discharge. He seemed unsettled toward any plans for
the future. He married a local young lady and completed two years
of college. He then opened his own business. Even after the birth of
three boys, he often seemed distant, would drift away in memories,
But his family supported him and loved him as they always had.

One of saddest tragedies occurred with the five Sullivan brothers
from Waterloo, Iowa. All of the brothers joined the navy and wished
to serve on the same ship. Their wish was granted, but on November
13, 1942, their ship was torpedoed by a Japanese submarine—all five
brothers perished. This struck a chord in the hearts of every citizen.
The sympathy for the remaining family was overwhelming. Following
that incident, never again were brothers placed together in the same

unit. Later, Hollywood made a movie about their lives and their ultimate sacrifice. The movie title is *The Fighting Sullivans.*

In the early part of 1943, a blimp hangar was built in Tillamook, a town just south of Seaside. This added another layer of protection for the coast of Oregon. Blimps flew low over the ocean, always on the lookout for submarines. It was very reassuring to hear the distinctive sound of their motors as they patrolled the shore. They flew daily over the beach and were quite picturesque, their silver color contrasting with the blue sky.

Every young lady wanted to look her very best when working at the USO or the Red Cross Center. However, Uncle Sam was now getting into the fashion business. To save yardage in women's and girls' clothing, the new rule for apparel was restricting hems to two inches, and no cuffs on dresses or blouses. The only exemptions were bridal gowns, maternity dresses, and vestments for religious orders.

Nylon stockings were nonexistent. The substitute was rayon, which was not as sheer or alluring. A brand new cosmetic appeared, stocking makeup. Young ladies were applying this new product and then painting a black line on the back of their legs to resemble the seams. From a distance, it looked like they were wearing nylon stockings. During the entire war years, this fad caught on and was very popular.

Wheatley's Dry Goods was the main source in town for sheets, towels, and basic clothing. The owners had a hard time keeping the shelves stocked with basic necessities. The residents flocked to the store when a new shipment arrived. Sheets, towels, and yardage were rationed; the number sold was dependent upon the family needs. The owners tried to be very fair about selling scarce items, and nearly everyone knew how hard it was for the store to deny someone an extra pair of sheets.

Labor Day approached and the summer season was over. Once again, summer residents cleaned their homes and packed belongings and left for the winter. Many stores along Broadway closed, with only the basic stores remaining open.

School started and the youngsters proved their patriotism by holding war-bond drives and by collecting paper and scrap metal. Football games became very popular, with the stands filled with soldiers and sailors. If they couldn't be home cheering for their own team, Seaside provided a sense of home for them.

As 1943 rolled on, the war was turning in favor of the Allies. The Japanese began to evacuate Guadalcanal. In September of that year, Italy surrendered. The Allied landed at Salerno to defeat the Germans occupied in Italy. Each victory brought a sense of relief to the town and a sense of optimism. By then, it looked like the Allies would defeat Hitler and gain victory over Japan. That was not the time to give up on all the efforts the town put into the war effort. War bonds were still sold at intermission at the Times Theater. Hollywood was still producing movies about the war and several light-hearted musicals that brought smiles to everyone.

The year 1944 saw many changes in the war. The Germans retreated from Leningrad, ending a 900-day siege. Over one million residents died from starvation and disease. Residents of the town were shocked with the news of the death toll. Russia was our friend, so we had supplied an airlift of food and medicine, but apparently the aid hadn't been enough to save many lives.

There was other war news that lifted the spirits of the town. Each bit of news was gratefully received. Guam was retaken by the US Army. Athens Greece was liberated. The Allies secured Southern France. General MacArthur returned to the Philippines, and all of our men and women were freed and returned home. A major bill was signed by President Roosevelt in June, the GI Bill, which offered financial and educational benefits to returning veterans. Once the war was over, servicemen and servicewomen could attend college and continue their education.

On the political front, in November, President Roosevelt defeated Thomas Dewey to win his unprecedented fourth term as President. Seaside remained unaware of how ill President Roosevelt really was. Most people thought it would be unwise to change horses in the middle of the stream, especially since the end of the war seemed to be very close.

In December 1944, the most shocking news reached Seaside. Glen Miller, the band leader, had enlisted in the army and was conducting his orchestra overseas for the men in service. He was a Major in the Army and boarded a plane from England to France; somewhere over the English Channel, the plane was brought down, and all men were presumed to have drowned. There was no trace of any survivors. Glen Miller was one of the greatest big-band leaders in the country. Whenever a band played "In the Mood," the song would inundate the listeners with memories of his band's great sound.

Christmas had a brighter feeling that year. Once again, families made all the preparations for a lovely holiday season. Mothers cooked traditional Christmas dinners, children still tried to snoop at presents, and stockings were hung. Churches were filled to capacity on Christmas Eve and Christmas Day. There was much more to be thankful for this season. The servicemen were invited to the homes of residents, to share a joyful and lovely holiday meal.

New Year's Day of 1945 dawned hopefully; this would be the year the war would end, when our troops would come home. The Allies were advancing into Germany. For years the residents of the town had heard rumors about the Nazi death camps. In January, Auschwitz was liberated, and everyone finally learned that the rumors were true.

Over six million Jews were killed, along with innumerable Gypsies and other ethnic groups. The town was horrified; the atrocity was beyond comprehension. What's more, Nazis had looted homes and taken valuable art and other possessions from the Jewish citizens. How long would it take to find these items and return them to their rightful owners? There would be so much work to do after the war.

In April, the town received the most devastating news of all: President Roosevelt had a massive heart attack and then passed on. When the news was delivered to the students at the high school, shock and disbelief prevailed. This was the only President whom these students had known. He had served from 1932 to 1945. Who would be the new President? What kind of leader would he be? Had President Roosevelt included him in any of the conferences and plans to bring the war to a successful conclusion? Only time would tell. Vice President Harry S. Truman was sworn in as the thirty-third president of the United States of America.

All war efforts were redoubled, as the end was in sight. Scrap metal, paper, and rubber goods were still being collected for the war. Women doubled their efforts at the defense plants. The Red Cross and USOs were filled to capacity because so many young men were being shipped overseas.

On May 7, 1945, the Germans were surrounded at General Eisenhower's headquarters. That part of the world was now at peace. Lights came on in all the major cities of Europe. Seaside, a grateful town, sighed in relief. All efforts could now focus on fighting Japan and freeing all of its prisoners of war. President Truman made a momentous decision to drop atomic bombs on Hiroshima and Nagasaki. This signaled an end to the war. On August 15, 1945, Japan announced its surrender. The country officially signed the documents on September 2, 1945. The war was over. The American,

battle-related deaths totaled 291,557. The estimated military and civilian deaths throughout the world numbered 55 million.

On August 15, the shadow lifted. The town went wild the day
Japan surrendered. The celebration was not quite as elaborate as in
the larger cities, but Seaside certainly was filled with great jubila-
tion. The siren sounded and the church bells joined the observance
of peace. People came out of their homes and banged pots and pans,
or created any type of noise that they could. Businesses closed on
Broadway. Soldiers and sailors danced in the middle of the street
with the local young ladies. The bars stayed open and did a land-
slide business. There were no more blackouts. Rationing ceased. No
more boys were being sent overseas. Curfews were lifted; lights were
turned on. Tillamook Lighthouse, after restoring its bright light,
shone proudly over the ocean. The festivities continued through the
night.

A more quiet celebration was held in all the local churches. People
prayed and thanked God, not only for the men and women who
would return home safely, but also for those who had died on foreign
shores. Gratitude and thanksgiving were expressed by all.

The Japanese who had been placed in internment camps were
released. Although the nice Japanese family who had lived in Seaside
was permitted to return to the West Coast, it did not return.

The townspeople knew their future would change again. Soon,
all the servicemen and their families would be returning to their
homes. Of course, Fort Stevens, Tongue Point Naval Air Station,
and Camp Rilea would stay in operation for a time, but with a reduced force.

The women, who had left their homes to do work for the Red
Cross and maintain the USO, would be free to be housewives again.
This did present problems because some women preferred to stay in
the workforce. Each family would have to sort out this situation.

The manufacturing plants returned to producing cars. Soon, people were trading in their older models, which had to last throughout the war years, for the newest and latest styles. Food was no longer rationed, and meat returned to the tables of families. The fishing fleet in Astoria was in full production.

Labor Day approached, and many stores closed for the winter. The merchants who stayed open during this time were busy ordering supplies. Once again, Wheatley's Dry Goods could supply residents with new sheets, towels, materials, shoes, and—most importantly—nylon stockings. The residents returned to their social events, such as bowling, community sings, club meetings, and movies.

The young men who had been drafted were returning home. Some aimed to complete high school, but most sought to enroll in college under the GI Bill. Universities were building new dorms for all of the returning servicemen. This pleased the young ladies, because now their social lives would improve at college.

At the start of high school in 1946, the senior class was busily planning lots of activities for the coming year. All of the students were looking forward to the football games. This was the first year they would play night games. Prior to this, all games were played in the afternoon in the field adjacent to the high school. For the people who would attend the games, the City had purchased lights for Broadway's field, bleachers, and parking spaces.

Vern Cook, coach at the high school, possessed outstanding football skills and knowledge of the game. The most important lesson he taught the players was excellent sportsmanship abilities. He always stressed the importance of quick thinking in playing good ball. It was the cooperation between Coach Cook and the players that made the team so successful.

That year turned out to be one of the best for Seaside's football team—it won every game it played. Perhaps the night games continually spurred them on to victory, but many townspeople felt pride in their hometown was the impetus. However, due to the way the teams were picked for the championship games, Seaside was not given the chance to participate and show Oregon what they could do. Quite a few of the young boys took with them the lessons Coach Cook had taught and went on to lead very successful lives in their respective careers.

Memorial Day 1947 arrived, and businesses were up and running again. Bungalow Dance Hall opened for the summer and filled to capacity every Saturday evening. It still could get the big bands to appear. Swing music was in style.

On July 12 of that summer, the headliner was Jimmie Lunceford. He had a master's degree in music. His band was ahead of its time, both in innovations and arrangements. This was one of the most popular bands at the Cotton Club in Harlan and was compared to Duke Ellington and Count Basie.

The rules for the band members were very strict. All had to conduct themselves with the upmost modesty and correctness. Their manner of dress had to be impeccable along with their decorum.

The band had played in southern states and were used to racial prejudice. It would be a relief to play in the Pacific Northwest and not be limited in where they could eat and sleep.

The evening before they were to appear in Seaside, they were scheduled to play in Portland. It was quite a shock to band members when they went to a restaurant right across from their venue, to have a bite to eat before starting their musical set. They waited patiently for their order to be taken; however, the waitress ignored them. Other patrons in the establishment who were white were delighted to see them and exchanged greetings.

After ten minutes, they requested service. The waitress informed them that the restaurant did not cater to people like them; she told them to leave. When they did not, she phoned the police and reported that they were causing a disturbance. Four policemen appeared to determine the extent of the problem. Immediately the other people stated they had not caused any trouble—they had only wanted to get food. The police informed the waitress she would have to serve the band or close the restaurant. The woman immediately placed the closed sign in the window.

The next day they boarded a bus for Seaside to play at the Bungalow Dance Hall. It was approximately 5:00 p.m. when they arrived. Mr. Lunceford told the band manager he was not feeling well, that his leg was sore and bothering him quite a bit. He was under some stress due to high blood pressure, and one of his severe headaches was growing. He stated he would see his doctor for a complete physical, once the band's tour ended.

After meeting the manager of the dance hall and setting up their instruments, some of the band members headed across the street to a small restaurant to have a bite to eat. There was a slight misunderstanding with the waitress. The men ordered hamburgers, which the restaurant didn't have. Thinking this might be a racial slight, Mr. Lunceford became very upset and lost his temper. He shouted and pounded the table, stating that they had a right to be served. The musicians had never seen him quite so upset. The incident was very quickly settled, and they were served hot roast beef sandwiches.

They returned to the dance hall, and Mr. Lunceford crossed the street to the record shop to sign some albums. He was accompanied by Joe Wilder and Al Cobbs, fellow musicians. While autographing, he asked for a glass of water. Upon reaching for the glass, he fell to the floor, where he lay unconscious. An ambulance was called, and he was transported to the local hospital. The musicians returned to the Bungalow Dance Hall but didn't say anything to the other men.

A little after 7:00 p.m., the band members began their set. The audience went wild. The first number was fast with an upbeat tempo, and most dancers stood around the bandstand just to listen. It was fabulous.

The band members couldn't understand why their leader hadn't yet arrived. At intermission, Kirkland Bradford left to make a phone call to the hospital. He was informed Mr. Lunceford had just passed away. The band members listened in disbelief. They didn't know what to do or what to think. Decisions had to be made quickly. Should they tell the audience? Should they continue to play that evening? What about the rest of the tour? They were due in Seattle the next evening, and that was the last stop of the Northwest tour.

When the band returned to the orchestra stage, Joe Thomas announced to the audience the sad news of Mr. Lunceford's untimely death. He had been forty-five, the winner of many prestigious awards, an icon of African American culture, and the inspiration for countless bandleaders and musicians.

His passing was a great tragedy. However, rumors started almost immediately. Could it have been foul play? Was he poisoned at the restaurant? Was this another example of racial prejudice?

The doctors in attendance at the hospital stated he had suffered a heart attack. That was the official reason listed on the death certificate. However, a few people persisted in perpetuating the rumor of foul play.

Shortly after, the band discontinued, and many found employment with other groups. Some of this information was obtained from "Rhythm is Our Business" by Eddy Determeyer. About forty years later, interviews with the few band members still alive revealed some discrepancies in their stories. However, the story told in the book is the most accurate description of this unfortunate event.

Tourism was low that summer, and the Chamber of Commerce took notice. It promptly formed a new committee that could both look into special events to attract visitors and create positive publicity for the community. This committee planned different activities that took place about every two weeks during the summer months. One of the accomplishments was applying to the franchise for the Miss America organization to create the Miss Oregon Pageant. The committee appointed Mr. M. C. Thorn as Master of Ceremonies, and Mrs. Thorn served as chairperson of the hostess committee. In February 1947, the head of the Miss America Pageant Hostess Committee visited the town and provided additional help and advice to the local committee.

This proved to be one of the most successful events staged in town. That evening, the entire auditorium of Central Grade School was filled with people cheering for their favorite contestant. The first ever Miss Oregon, crowned in 1947, was Jo Ann Amorde, Miss Sutherland. She placed in the top fifteen finalists in the Miss America contest that year. The event was received quite well, and the town felt that it had solved one of its problems concerning the city's diminished tourism.

Many other young ladies, in the following years, placed in the top ten finalists, with some becoming the first runner-ups. In 2001, the ultimate prize was won. Katie Harman, Miss Portland, was crowned Miss America. This certainly gave the state of Oregon and Seaside much publicity. Katie appeared at several events in the city following her reign as the winner. The event is now titled Miss Oregon Scholarship Pageant and held in July each summer.

CHAPTER 2

1950S

THE NEW DECADE STARTED OUT quite well for the small town. Tourists flocked to the beach during the summer. With many people purchasing new automobiles (the rationing of gas had ended), everyone could spend vacations and weekends away from home. Most of the amusement places were still running, and the town always had a carnival atmosphere in the summer. However, there were changes taking place.

In January, the town hosted Olsen's Red Heads Female Basketball Team. They were to play the Seaside Elks Basketball Team, BPOE. Yes, women playing against men in a sports activity. This was very progressive for the '50s. Furthermore, they played by the men's rules. In high schools and colleges, women played under different guidelines. Due to the medical information of the day, it was thought to be unwise for women to run full court. As a result, women's games were played half court, with three players on each side. So here was an innovation for women.

This was the world's tallest women's team, averaging five feet nine inches tall, with five of the women being over six feet. The team not only played a wicked game of basketball against all of its opponents, but during halftime, the team showed off its ability to do trick shooting. The first half of the game went strictly by the rules. However, after a wonderful halftime show, trick shooting was the name of the game. The women were fabulous at this game. Many hours of practice had made them experts at shooting and dribbling the ball. The men often lost track of which player had the ball until a shot was made. Then all they could do was shake their heads in disbelief.

One of the star players, Lorene, would sink to her knees during halftime and shoot foul shots—sometimes making as many as fifty in a row. The crowd loved it. What's more, the team always played to a sold-out audience. Of course, most of the audience was supposed to cheer for the Seaside Elks team, but that quickly changed because the women outdid themselves in playing. It was obvious that BPOE didn't stand for Best Players on Earth. The women outscored and outshot the men. After the game was completed, the men showed good sportsmanship by congratulating the women and giving them a standing ovation.

The Red Heads were so popular that they had three teams. They existed from 1936 to 1966, appearing on many of the hit television shows of the day. Events like this were always welcome and provided relief for the dark, raining evenings.

In January, the Mayor signed a contract with the Duncan Parking Meter Company to install meters on Broadway. It was stated in the agreement that after twelve months, the meters could be removed at no cost to the city. People could park for two hours; however, as long as a person continually fed a meter, he or she could stay in the same spot all day.

In February, the weather played a trick on the town. It was recorded as the worst winter in history. There was ice on the Necanicum River, and the temperature was 11½ degrees. There was five inches of snow in one day, and the month of January recorded 23½ feet of snow.

Other changes were going on in the town. Utilities would be placed underground on Broadway to beautify the town center.

Work started on a new drive-in theater just north of Seaside, in Gearhart. Complete with a snack center and a screen that was fifty-by-sixty feet, the theater opened on May 5, capable of holding 530 cars. The first movie shown was *Canadian Pacific Railroad*, starring the very popular Randolph Scott. It was quite successful because people could now take their children with them and relax in their cars. No longer did parents have to worry about small children disturbing other patrons during the show.

Some citizens were concerned that the needs of the people were not being met, so town meetings were held to discuss various problems. The first item for discussion was the hospital. A committee was established to work closely with the staff to find solutions that would benefit everyone. The hospital was vital to the community, for both the residents and tourists. The committee worked diligently with the medical staff to ensure everything went orderly and professionally.

For the first time in history, the Seaside Gulls would participate in the State Basketball Tournament. A victory over Tillamook clinched spot for the team. This was quite an accomplishment for the small town, and everyone was quite proud of the team. The boys lost their first game to Scappoose by a score of forty-six to forty-one. However, this did not damper the enthusiasm of the local townspeople for their team.

Also making news in the sports scene was Marv Diercks, a graduate of the class of 1947. Playing on the football and basketball teams, he had been a very popular figure in high school. After two years at Portland University, he was signed with the Portland Beavers, one of the teams in the Pacific Coast League. They were owned by the Chicago Cubs. At spring training in Riverside, California, the Beavers were playing the Cubs and getting very strongly trounced. Toward the end of the game, the manager put Marv in as a pinch hitter. After two swings at the ball, he connected and hit a home run.

Marv told his family after the game that he was so shocked that he could only stand there on home plate as the ball soared over the fence. The catcher had to tell him that he was supposed to run around the bases, which he did with great joy and happiness. The homerun was the only score in the game for the Beavers. Marv played for two years with farm teams until he was drafted into the Army.

Another athletic young man from the town was Ken Carpenter, a graduate of Seaside High school in 1944. He played football for Oregon State between 1946 and 1949. The Cleveland Browns picked him as a first-round draft choice. He played for the Browns from 1950 to 1953; during that time, the team won one NFL championship and played in three more. Ken was named to the Pro-Bowl in 1951.

In 1954, he joined the Canadian Football League and signed with the Roughriders. Later in 1955, he led the league in scoring. He was named a divisional all-star in 1955, 1956, and 1958. In 1960, he played for the Denver Broncos. Injuries were slowing him down, so he became a coach for various teams. After retiring from football, Ken worked as head of recreation at the Indiana Department of Correction. He was inducted into the Oregon Sports Hall of Fame in 1982 and into Oregon State's Hall of Fame in 1991.

The town did not forget its young ladies. Their beauty, talent, and dedicated work was paying off. Miss Rae Hardisty was selected as Grand Worthy Advisor of the Grand Assembly of Rainbow Girls. Also, Donna Manion was elected as Grand Chaplin. These young ladies were selected for their devotion to the Order of Rainbow Girls. It was quite an honor to have two Grand Officers from Maple Assembly 30. They were installed in their posts in front of over two thousand people attending the ceremony. They both served admirably for their terms.

A tall, blond beauty, Gloria McCulley, was elected as Miss Ice Cream and reigned over the ice cream manufacturers' convention held in Gearhart. That same year, she represented Gearhart in the Miss Oregon pageant. She was also a model at Meier Frank's department store in Portland. She was not only lovely but also one of the nicest girls in her high school class; she was very popular with everyone.

The town felt that, with the growth being made, the Chamber of Commerce building should be finished in time for the summer season. However, funds were a little short for the completion of the task.

Bill Daggett, one of the owners of The Crab Broiler (one of the popular eating establishments), stepped up to the plate and personally saw to financing the completion of the buildings inside area. The chamber was very grateful to Bill for taking on this task. Once the construction was completed, the town had a central building in which important activities could be planned.

In the same year, another improvement occurred in the town. Dan Callahan, manager of the Strand Theater, purchased new sound equipment. The technology was ultramodern, resulting in the voices and music in films taking on lifelike qualities. Also, the movie theater received a new paint job inside and new seats, to the cost of $3,500. This made quite a difference in the older of the two theaters in town.

In March 1950, the town was reminded of the war. A small aerial bomb, two feet long by four inches in diameter, was found on the beach, south of the mouth of the river. It was turned over to the closest Coast Guard station, and it disposed of the bomb's remains.

The big bands began to lose their popularity when rock and roll was growing and taking over the country. The teenagers were no longer jitterbugging but instead inventing new dances. Stars like Elvis Presley and Carl Perkins were the idols of the day.

Suddenly, the Bungalow Dance Hall was no longer the place to go. Sadly, it closed and became a roller-skating rink for a few years. Eventually, skating fell out of style, resulting in the old dance hall being torn down. For all of the servicemen and young people who had grown up in the '40s, it was a very sad day.

The new homes being built no longer had front porches on which residents could sit in the evening hours or could host the visits of their friends. New people moving into the communities had a hard time meeting their neighbors. Gone were the visiting times, the swapping of recipes, and the catching up on everything going on in the town. The young people no longer played hide-and-seek, kick-the-can, or stickball in the streets.

Television arrived. Many homes boasted a new black-and-white set. Entertainment was now coming into people's homes. This gave a new dynamic to the family setting. Instead of gathering around the radio, everyone would huddle around the televisions. News was up to date, and people could watch the latest variety shows. Arthur Godfrey and Ed Sullivan were seen every Thursday and Saturday evening. Their shows hosted the best variety acts that could be found. Essentially, their shows were an updated vaudeville show. Of course, some residents missed the visiting of neighbors, but now the family environment easily received entertainment and gossip, thanks to the arrival of television sets.

During the day, housewives could watch *Queen for a Day*, *The Price Is Right*, and many other television shows. Although the sets only had twelve channels, having a television was very exciting. Radio started to become a thing of the past. Not everyone was impressed with this new type of entertainment, and some die-hards held on to their radios.

Wrestling was one of the most watched sports. Individuals such as Gorgeous George, Baron Leonne, and Roger Mackey were just a few of the names that families loved to cheer or boo. Most of the drama was phony, but these stars did put on quite a show. As in the old Western movies, the strong and handsome heroes fought the notorious villains. The heroes didn't always win, but there was always the next match—in which they could prove that good conquers evil.

Roller derby came alive on the television screens. Each team had stars who were clever in getting publicity. Teams were either known for playing by the rules or for having several underhanded tricks for the game. It was great entertainment, but the outcomes of the matches were possibly staged.

On June 25, 1950, North Korea invaded South Korea; once again, war threatened the small town. In July 1950, American troops joined the fight in behalf of the South Korea Army. General MacArthur, Commander of the US Armed Forces, felt that if the North Korea Army succeeded in its invasion, Russian Communists would proceed to invade any country they wanted. President Truman had a different view and fired General MacArthur. It was not called a war but a police action. It ended in July 1953—but not before forty thousand American Troops were killed, with another one hundred thousand left wounded. Total fatalities numbered over five million individuals. One of those men killed in action was from Seaside. The town mourned the loss of one of its residents and continued to pray that there would be no more wars.

Seaside was growing in population and boundaries. Seaside Heights was developed, and various lots were purchased for new homes. Cornet, Safeway, and The Ocean Vista Shopping Center proudly boasted new buildings. Parking meters were installed on Broadway and proved quite profitable.

The Jeffery Estate controlled most of the business property on Broadway, as a result of the Grimes donation for the land claim. Because this land was sold, business owners on Broadway could think about permanent and improved buildings. This was a welcomed addition to the town. The rejuvenation of Broadway could be more realistically pursued.

The end of the summer season was excellent. The Seaside Signal reported such headlines as "Business Volume High" and "Season Business Good." The progress of the city indicated that finances were in excellent shape. All in all, things seemed to be going very well.

Most of the entertainment centers had been torn down; this meant there were less things for the young people to do. However, the beach remained a popular spot. In those days, individuals were not worried about suntans causing serious skin damage. Getting as brown as possible was still a desirable situation.

An article in the Seaside Signal appeared on November 24, 1955, informing its readers that the newspaper would carry a complete listing of all the programs on three television stations. At that time, Seaside could only secure ABC, NBC, and CBS. Nevertheless, television was entertainment and proved a diversion for rainy evenings.

One of the saddest days in the '50s was the decommissioning of the Tillamook Rock Lighthouse, also known as Terrible Tilly. It was built in 1878, and its light had proudly shown throughout all of its years. It had been turned off only once, the evening the Japanese submarine shelled the coast of Oregon.

During the long, dark winter nights, to look out upon the ocean and see the light shining was reassuring. Many times during the summer evenings, people would sit on the Prom and watch the light gleaming across the water. It represented safety and security.

The lighthouse had a very difficult start, and many people believed that to build such a structure along the coast would be impossible. The government decided this particular part of the ocean needed more light to assist the ships that were rounding the Tillamook Head. There was no place to erect a lighthouse on the land. Tillamook Head could not hold such a massive construction. The only spot was a rock 1.2 miles offshore. So the builders set about building the lighthouse on the most impractical, unfeasible place—Tillamook Rock.

In 1879, when John Trewavas, a surveyor, attempted to land on the rock, his foot slipped; he was swept into the ocean, never to be seen again. This was one of many deaths on the place.

A team of quarrymen managed to complete the task in 575 days. They had to rig a line between the ship and top of the rock to transport both their tools and themselves to the place of construction. As men rode across the water in the bucket, large waves would often splash them with frigid ocean water. Shortly before the lighthouse was completed, the ship *Lupatia* sailed too close to the shore in a heavy fog. The next morning, the bodies of all the crew had washed up on the rock.

The eighty-by-forty-five foot building was designed to hold four keepers, all men, and it was forbidden to bring along wives and children. It was indeed a forsaken place. A few keepers could not stand the isolation and had to be removed from the lighthouse. The keepers soon learned what loneliness was all about.

Sam Churchill noted the 1934 storm and wrote,

The crew barely was lashed to the rock before the first storm hit and clung to life by the slimmest of margins as winds and water clawed at them in an effort to sweep them into the sea. Tons of water, broken glass, rocks, dead fish, seaweed, and barnacles came pouring down the throat of the tower flooding the interior and forcing men to climb the rafters to keep heads above water. It was then they realized Tillamook Rock Light Station, including the light tower, 133 feet above the sea, was under water (quote taken from "Terrible Tilly by Bert and Margie Webber).

In 1957, after it was decommissioned by the US Coast Guard, the last keeper wrote the following statement about his time as a keeper:

Farewell Tillamook Rock Light Station, an era has ended with this final entry and without sentiment. I return thee to the elements. Then, one of the most notorious and yet most fascinating of the sea Sentinels in the world—long the friend of the tempest-tossed mariner. Through howling gale, thick fog and driving rain your beacon has been a star of hope and your fog horn a voice of encouragement. May the elements of nature be kind to you. For 77 years you have beamed your light across desolate acres of ocean. Keepers have come and gone; men have lived and died, but you were faithful to the end. May your sunset years be good years. Your purpose to now only symbol, but the lives you have saved and the service you have rendered is worthy of the highest respect. A protector of life property to all, may old timers, newcomers and travelers along the way pause from the shore in memory of your humanitarian role. He h"9-19-57 Oswalk Allik, keeper.

One of the highlights of the year for the young boys was the Boy Scout Jamboree held in Valley Forge, Pennsylvania. Henry Dessler coordinated the effort to raise money for the local boys who wished to attend. Once again, the town rallied together to supply money and equipment for the scouts. The American Legion donated $450, the Kiwanians $300, and the Local Carpenters Union $300. It would cost $300 to send each boy on the road trip, with a tour scheduled for Washington, DC. Approximately forty thousand Boy Scouts from all over the world attended. When the three Seaside boys and their chaperons returned home, they told amazing tales of their adventures and new friendships.

Fun events were held in the winter months to assist the locals in enduring the long, rainy evenings. One of these events was staged by the Gull-outs, a division of the Chamber of Commerce. This was a spoof on the Miss America Pageant. With several members dressed in women's evening gowns, they appeared on the stage. After much laughter from the audience, Paul Scoggins won with a rousing rendition of Alice Blue Gown. His prize was on hundred dollars. It was a hilarious burlesque on the more serious Miss America Pageant.

The Seaside Signal announced that the school would be recruiting three new teachers for the coming year, bringing the total staff to fifteen. Salaries were also given. Women were to be paid $3,000 to $3,500, while men teachers were paid $4,000 to $4,500. Discrepancies in pay between men and women were a fact of life, and no one fought against this unfairness openly. The thoughts of the women teachers were not printed in the paper.

In May, an open house was held at the hospital. The write-up in the paper described the institution as a hotel with twenty-four-hour room service, a restaurant that can provide all kinds of meals, plus twenty-eight adult beds, and two children and two bassinets for the youngest residents of the town. On the average, it housed thirteen patients full-time. There were 428 operations and 137 births. It would appear those bassinets were full a great deal of the time.

However, the aquarium was not quite so lucky with its mortality rate. The first seal pup born in captivity did not survive. His mother and father were Flipper and Nappy. However, learning from this experience, the curator continued the breeding process and was the first to successfully breed a harbor seal in a controlled environment.

The l950s came to an end. Many of the merchants expressed concern for how the town would hold the interest of tourists in the coming decade.

CHAPTER 3

1960s

─────

ALTHOUGH THE 1960S BROUGHT SOME improvement to the town, it also proved to be the start of the downward trend for the beloved resort.

The '60s, all across the nation, were known as the most radical, turbulent times for any town to live through. It brought a mixture of good and extremely difficult circumstances. It started out with John F. Kennedy becoming President of the United States. Many people were delighted to see a young family in the White House. Newscasters referred to this time as the Golden Era. How quickly it became tarnished. The young President was assassinated on November 22, 1963. The country was in shock and mourned greatly for this popular young president. He left a young widow and two small children. There were many changes to come in the years ahead.

The town was reeling because of all the ups and downs. The big bands and the mellow music of the '40s vanished; rock and roll was suddenly the only thing young people listened to. Protest songs were in vogue. Young people were questioning the standard methods of teaching and learning. They wanted more than the old ways of doing things. Sex, drugs, and rock and roll were popular slogans of the decade. Everyone seemed to have a reason to fight against the "establishment." Civil rights and women's rights became the most popular movements.

With so many entertainment centers demolished, there was little for the young people to do in Seaside, except gather on Broadway in large groups. Labor Day weekend 1962 was the pivotal point for the town. All it took was a mixed crowd of young people, some liquor, and a few instigators to produce a recipe for disaster—disaster with a capital D. The town was almost completely destroyed by a riot of college and teenage youths.

According to the police, the riot had been brewing all weekend, starting Saturday evening around 6:00 p.m. The unruly crowd took down the tall lifeguard tower, which had proudly stood on the beach, and carried it down Broadway. Within seconds, the crowd turned wild. The Seaside Fire Department arrived on the scene and began shoving the crowd back to the beach with fire hoses. The mentality of the herd took over. Blindly obeying each other, the young people hurled rocks, bricks, and broken beer bottles at the police. Fire hoses were cut. Store windows were smashed.

Nothing was safe. Stores and restaurants immediately emptied out and more youths joined the fracas. The Seaside police department was outnumbered. Help arrived from the various cities bordering the town, but the aid was not enough to put an immediate stop to the chaos, which morphed into a full-scale riot between the young people and authorities.

For seven hours, the battle raged up and down Broadway. The State Police joined the embattled Seaside police force. Police, standing back to back, supported each other; they had to stand tall—falling would lead to a more severe beating. Dodging rock, bricks, and anything that could be thrown, the police bravely defended the town. One picture in the local newspaper said it all: a police officer, with blood streaming down his face, was arresting a rioter. Another picture was of a volunteer fireman examining a slashed fire hose. This was just one of many items that were damaged. By the time the first phase was over, more than one hundred rioters had been arrested, fifty were in jail, and thirteen were hospitalized. It was approximately 1:00 a.m. before the authorities had full control of the situation. Thirteen people, including two policemen, a fireman, and ten students were injured.

The sale of alcoholic beverages was banned from Warrenton to Arch Cape. The ban would be lifted Tuesday, according to the State Liquor Commission.

During Sunday night, two buses with National Guard aboard made trips to Astoria, transporting some of the prisoners from the small Seaside jail to the Astoria jail.

By Sunday morning, many of the family visitors were leaving town, stating that they didn't feel safe after the riot. This was certainly a loss of revenue to the businesses.

On Sunday, the crowd of youths started again, this time threating to storm the jail and release their friends. By now the State Police, armed with ax handles and baseball bats, chased the crowd to the beach. Armed National Guardsman looked on from the roof tops, ready to join the State Police, if necessary.

Once on the beach, two local men, Dick Rankin and Joe Camberg, started playing guitars. As the crowd became orderly, they organized entertainment, some of it provided by the rioters. The rock and roll band The Wailers arrived and played nonstop for four hours. Several of the town's residents were quite vocal about the band playing on the beach. The townspeople felt the young people were being rewarded for their misbehavior. It raised quite a discussion in the Signal and the City Council meeting.

The National Guard stayed on their post, and the Seaside Police Department patrolled Broadway. That seemed to be the end of the rioting for the weekend. But this was the start of trouble for this once happy small town. By Tuesday, the merchants had cleaned up their shops, assessed the damages; some closed for good, feeling that many of the tourists would not return next year. The total cost to the town was $2,027 in overtime for police, firemen, and extra policemen from other cities.

The Chamber of Commerce held a meeting immediately following the weekend to study the problem and determine the solution. If Seaside wanted families to return in future summer, the town needed to project a safer image. It was time to erase the pictures of youths rioting and vandalizing the town. There was a great deal of work to be done. The town rolled up its sleeves and tried to find solutions to the problem.

During the winter months, various groups and organizations met to solve the challenges of changing the image of the town. Broadway started to look like it had forgotten how to clean itself up. Store fronts needed a new coat of paint, streets needed sweeping, and the town gradually sunk into despair.

If that wasn't enough bad news, on March 27, 1964 (Good Friday), a large earthquake hit Alaska. The result was a tsunami off the Pacific Northwest Coast. Tsunamis were rare. Most of the citizens were unaware of safety precautions necessary for survival.

Previously in January 1700, a 9.2 earthquake in Japan precipitated a large tsunami off the coast of the town. At that time, some of the Clatsop Native Americans were living on the beach. When the waters receded, they ran out into the surf to collect clams and other seafood. Suddenly, a very large, powerful wave descended on them, and many lives were lost. There is no record of how many died in this tragedy, but an individual can easily imagine the confusion and despair at that time. Fortunately, Japan had devices that measured the earthquake and some written history of tsunamis.

This tsunami in 1964 was different. Instead of coming in from the ocean, it ran through the rivers in town. A ten-foot wave traveled down the Necanicum River, destroying the Fourth Street Bridge. Every bridge that crossed the river, except the Broadway and Avenue U bridges, were damaged.

Cars were pushed into houses along the banks. Trees were knocked over, some falling on small beach cabins. As usual, everyone stopped to help those who were in trouble. People looked after their neighbors. For those individuals who couldn't drive, people just loaded their cars with as many people as possible and headed for higher ground.

Most citizens drove to Sunset Hills, where residents opened their homes to all, providing shelter and assistance. The situation was a wake-up call for the town. After the danger was over, many people partied with the residents of Sunset Hills.

How does a community prepare itself for this type of emergency? Fortunately, no one was killed, but there was property damage adding up to approximately $40,000. Here was a subject for the City Council to investigate, for which it would hopefully find solutions.

Today, every coastal town has warning signs posted that show the way to higher ground. Special sirens sound warnings of an approaching tsunami. Drills are practiced monthly. The town is well prepared for any emergency that may occur.

The one defining situation that occurred in the turbulent '60s was the Vietnam War, dividing not only families but also the nation. The slogan for the youth was "Hell no, we won't go!" This was repeated on high school and college campuses across the country.

We were asking our young men and women to cross the ocean and fight for a country and a cause that was not entirely defined. Our veterans, who had so gladly gone to battle in World War II, could not understand why the young were protesting. Our young people could not see the reason for this battle, and the division was bitter. Many of our youths fled to Canada instead of going into the Army.

The war began in 1954 but escalated in 1964—so did the protests. The nation was horrified and didn't seem to know how to settle this problem. Our country was working under the domino theory. If one country fell to the Communist Regime, many others would follow. By 1962, the military presence in South Vietnam had reached some nine thousand troops. This was in sharp contrast to the military presence being less than 800 in the 1950s. By June 1964, eighty-two thousand troops were stationed in Vietnam.

Television brought the war into the front room of every American home. Everyone could see the destruction, not only of lives but also of property. For many people, seeing the war up close and personal was horrific. Antiwar protests continued to grow, especially on college campuses. On November 15, 1969, the largest event was held peacefully, with over 250,000 citizens calling for the withdrawal of American troops from Vietnam.

The lives of many American families were plunged into despair as the casualty count mounted. Here in the small town, six local young men lost their lives in the conflict. There is a tribute paid to them in front of the library. Karl Marlantes, a resident of Seaside, wrote the definitive book on the war in Vietnam and his experiences, entitled *Matterhorn*. He wrote candidly about his struggle with post-traumatic stress disorder and was a vocal advocate for veterans suffering from the disorder. It remained on the best-seller list for several months. The town was quite proud of his accomplishment.

The sense of uneasiness toward the war seemed to spark other protests about racial inequality and equal pay for women. The country seemed to be in disarray about these issues, the disorder trickling down to every small town in the United States. Although Seaside had no industry or manufacturing plants, the subject of equal pay for women and equality for all races echoed throughout the town.

The war ended eventually, and many of the veterans returned to the opposite of a hero's welcome. The protesters called them baby killers and other names. Many of the young men and women who had fought so bravely were afraid to even declare they had been in Vietnam. There seemed to be no peaceful solution to this war. Even the end of hostilities didn't bring a sense of harmony. The small town worried as to what affect this would have on our nation. The churches in town were once again a healing place for many citizens.

On June 16, 1960, it was decided by the Chamber of Commerce to honor the Lewis and Clark expedition, which had occurred 145 years ago. Seaside claims to be the end of Lewis and Clark's trail—why not have a celebration to honor the history of the area?

The city would celebrate the expedition, bringing thousands of tourists into town for the weekend. There were horse races, beach runs, and canoe races on the Necanicum River. Also, a parade took place down Broadway. The Gull-outs were a major help in putting all of this on. The horse show was particularly entertaining and drew a large crowd of spectators. There was also a whisker contest for the longest and shortest beards, trimmed and trained. The entire event was to be topped off by a street dance, but unfortunately it was rained out. However, the rain didn't damper the spirit of the town and its visitors; the entire event ended up being a success. All of the money earned from the event would be used to build a fence around Broadway's park and bleachers.

CHAPTER 4

1970S

———

IN L974, THE TOWN LOST another of its old landmarks. Central Grade
School, which had stood for sixty years, was boarded up. All students
were transferred to the new elementary school at Seaside Heights after
Christmas vacation.

Gone was the old auditorium that had housed all graduations,
senior plays, and the Miss Oregon Pageant. The new grade school
provided larger class rooms and new technology to the students, but it
lacked the mellowness of the old school. The two-story brick building
had withstood so much in the way of wind, rain, and sleet—it just
seemed safer and stronger than the new buildings. Progress was the
word of the day: it was important for the youngsters to have the very
best in the way of education.

Many residents fondly remembered the old curtain that for so
long had hung on the stage of the auditorium. It was a painted picture
of the beach, ocean, and Tillamook Head. What memories the old
school held of all the events that had taken place in the old auditorium, which for years had been the gathering place for so many town
activities, graduations, community sings, and school plays.

If an individual were to pass by the old boarded-up building and
listen closely, he or she might hear the ghostly laughter of youngsters
playing in the school yard. Perhaps one may hear the groans of dismay

that would erupt when it was time to head back to class—possibly to face a test—or, even worse, the principal's office, especially if a student had been found guilty of an infraction of the rules. The principal had a strap in his office, and he would yield it if he had committed an offense.

By 1986, the building was an eyesore to the residents; they implored the City Council to have it demolished. The new owners had been trying to sell the building for quite some time, but the price of repairing it was prohibitive. Undoubtedly, it was filled with asbestos and lead paint. Removing asbestos requires a specialized firm, so that it does not escape into the air. Finally, the owners, exhausted from all of the appeals, agreed to the demolition.

In 1974, another event took place that brought publicity to the town. At the Miss Oregon Pageant, Juli Ann Berg was crowned the winner and prepared for her trip to Atlantic City for the Miss America contest. Her victory was unique for a particular reason: her mother, Jo Ann Berg, won the first Miss Oregon contest in 1947. Seldom has a mother and daughter had the good fortune to both represent a state in such a manner.

This was the year a television studio decided to film a series using Seaside as the first location. It was entitled *Moving On* and stared Claude Akins and Frank Converse. In the show, two independent truckers were traveling through the United States. In the first episode, another character (played by the actor Michael Pollard) had an accident. After being taken to a hospital, he learned that he had cancer. Upon learning of the man's disease, the two independent truckers decided to take him along and tour the country. What's more, Miss Oregon 1972 and Miss Oregon 1974 both had speaking parts in the film. The show debuted in September of that year on NBC.

Claude Akins was very popular with the citizens of Seaside. He was extremely friendly and known to have stated many times how much he loved the town. He was especially impressed with the beauty of the surrounding hills and the pristine beach.

By then, the town was in need of an overhaul, with its dirty streets and forlorn appearance. The summers were still packed with tourists but, unfortunately, not the types of visitors the town generally appreciated. Families were no longer looking to Seaside as a destination for a summer vacation. The riots had taken a toll on visitors. Most of the people who visited the town were young people, who just wanted to party and have a good time. There wasn't enough for them to do, and this was an open invitation for trouble.

It was time to do something. Once again, the town came together, and solutions were given on how to solve the problem. Families were the lifeblood of any resort community. It was imperative they return to vacation in this lovely resort town.

How to attract families to town? Here the Chamber of Commerce would play a very important part. Partnerships were set up between the City Council, Chamber and Parks and Recreation District. The city center needed to be revitalized. Streets cleaned and buildings painted. A more inviting and welcoming appearance was the order of the day.

The Seaside Hotel had been demolished and in its place stood a modern building, The Shilo Inn. The old hotel had stood for years just to the north of the turnaround. In its heyday, it had been a gracious place to reside, with its wide green lawn and portico filled with flowers. To lounge in its lobby, while sipping a glass of ice tea and watching the ocean, was a pleasant way to spend an afternoon.

The Shilo Inn provided an additional 113 rooms for visitors, an indoor swimming pool, and an oceanfront restaurant, as well as a full-service bar and meeting rooms on the lower level. A welcome addition to the town—but would the inn be enough to entice families back to town for summer vacations? There was so much more work to be done.

The natatorium had been closed down, and the building was then demolished. The only places where residents could swim were the ocean, private pools, or motel pools. None of these were good choices. It was now decided the town desperately needed a swimming pool for all residents. A drive was started to build a community pool; funds came from the PTA, baked-food sales, and donations from individuals. It soon became apparent that this would never provide sufficient funds for the project, The Sunset Park and Recreation District was authorized by the voters, thereby enabling the district to levy taxes.

Several locations were considered for this project. Eventually it was decided to build a pool in Broadway Park. This was the ideal location because Broadway Park and the riverfront were being developed. Mary Blake was hired as General Manager in 1984 and served in this position until June 2012. With her dynamic leadership, Sunset Empire Parks and Recreation begin to grow and develop into a project the town would be very proud of. People always knew when Mary was around by the ear splitting whistle she used to call attention to projects around the park. She had a vibrant, effervescent spirit that was felt by all. She also emphasized cooperative programming and special events, both recreational and aquatic.

Some of the first events held by the District was the Sunset Thriller, a haunted house around the pool. This was linked to a Seaside School District event by the "Ghost Bus." A television debut was held with a swimsuit fashion show done in historic Janzen suits and shown on a local educational program.

A problem the city faced were skateboarders on the Prom and Broadway. What was the answer to this growing concern about safety? A skateboard park, adjacent to the district building. There was also interest in the installation of a hot tub pool, and soon the two projects were combined. Donations were received from several local agencies and private citizens.

The District, cities of Seaside, and Astoria began to make plans for activities for the summer and fall. These included some sand games, a live rock-and-roll program, the rededication of the Prom, and some cultural programs. These activities could be the answer to one of the town's problems: they would provide more events to young people.

There were many challenges to be met during this time, but with dynamic leadership, all were accomplished. Today, the building includes all types of events for the citizens of the town.

The youngsters were not forgotten in the planning. The District has a childcare center for children from six weeks old to five years old, preschool, afterschool programs, holiday camps, free drop-in programs, Easter egg hunts, Christmas programs, and many more activities for the youths.

The Sunset Parks and Recreation District has been a blessing to the City. The building has a large swimming pool, a Youth Center, a large recreation room, and two small rooms for activities. The District also provides staffing for the Senior Center, which conducts numerous events during the year for the retired citizens. Also, many organizations rent the main room for their activities.

It was during this same time frame that the City realized the need for a Convention Center to attract events year round. A newly built convention center was sound in many ways and would have a positive economic result for the town. However, financing was the main problem to this enterprise. Would a unique partnership be the answer? Here again the city came together to solve the problem.

A committee was appointed, headed by Floyd Davis (the Chamber of Commerce President) and Henry Dessler. The two men made a study of the needs of the city, and how these could be met in the best manner. Also, a survey of the business district determined whether it would support an increase in license fees sufficient to retire bonds.

The result of this investigation showed that 94 percent of businesses favored the proposal.

A building committee was appointed, which consisted of Byron Meek, Michael Maki, Larry Haller, Ken Grant, and Warren Kan. They were asked to study what would be the general use of the building, in regard to conventions, education, entertainment, and the Miss Oregon Pageant, as well as the size necessary for all the activities.

A ballot measure was passed by 68 percent to borrow $300,000, which would be provided by General Obligation Bonds, resulting in the purchase of the bonds by the US National Bank at 5.9 percent interest. The project was started in 1970 and completed in 1971.

In 1978, the Convention Center was remodeled to add an entryway, foyer, and office, resulting in an additional seating capacity of 150 people. In 1986, a balcony was completed, which increased the seating by an extra 450 seats. The Convention Center can now hold 2,400 people comfortably.

The last expansion was completed in 1995; it increased the square footage to sixty-two thousand. Building usage has tripled since 1989 because it gained the ability to do concurrent events by using the additional space. It has indeed been a blessing to the community. The Convention Center continues to serve its purpose and has successfully met the needs of the town. It has indeed been a tremendous boost to the economic conditions in Seaside.

The Seaside Museum and Historical Society are located off Broadway on Necanicum Drive. It houses most of the information about the history of this lovely beach town. There, an individual may find a walking-tour map of the historical Seaside Prom homes, with information as to who the original owners were and when the homes were built. Some of the fine, older homes are bungalows and Victorians, and a few are examples of the Queen Ann style. This mixture of homes gives the Prom its unique look.

Adjacent to the museum building is the Butterfield Cottage. In the summer of 1888, many people were arriving in Seaside to spend their vacations. Tourists would first arrive near Warrenton and then would take the train to Seaside. Accommodations were needed for the summer influx of people.

Mr. Grimes, a local resident, built a hotel on the Necanicum River, but the size of the hotel could not accommodate all of the visitors. He then started to build tent platforms among the trees, and this became known as Grimes Grove.

Some people wanted more permanent housing for their vacations. Among them was Mr. Horace Seely Butterfield, a prominent jeweler in Portland. In 1893, he commissioned the Butterflied Cottage to be erected for his family.

The cottage has had many additions over the years and was used as the Butterfield's beach cottage until 1903; by then, the Butterfields had built five new places on the oceanfront.

In 1912, Mrs. Emelia Bitterling became caretaker of Butterfield Cottage and operated it as a rooming house in the summer. The small cottage had many modern features for its day, such as electric lights and a washing machine for clothes.

In 1958, Marion Roberts rented the cottage and opened a millinery shop. In 1972, it became an antique store.

On December 5, 1984, it was given to the Seaside Museum and moved to its present location. The museum people lovingly restored the cottage to its original condition as a beach home and rooming house. This is the only cottage that has survived from the original Grimes Grove. This small example of the early years of the town is a must see for all individuals who come to visit.

The museum proudly hosts a Social on the fourth of July, along with a silent auction, food booths, and many games for children of all ages. It is one of the highlights of the holiday.

Gingerbread Tea was a welcome addition to the town over the Christmas season. After decorating the Butterfield Cottage with old-fashion ornaments and garland, a lovely afternoon tea is served. A musician is employed to play appropriate music. Mothers, grandmothers, and grandchildren are often seen enjoying home-baked gingerbread with coffee, tea, or hot chocolate. A marvelous and relaxing way to participate in an afternoon and reminisce on days gone by.

If an individual toured the museum, he or she will find artifacts of years past. There is a dedication to Jenny Michel and her intricate weavings. The museum has a diorama of the town in the early 1900s, a spot for visitors to enjoy the Lewis and Clark men extracting salt, and a history of the Lattie family and its importance to the town. It is well worth the time to explore the building of the Seaside Museum and Historical Society.

The town is very proud of the museum. It is a depository for all of its history. People can study wonderful displays of the early Native Americans, the Clatsop Nation. They were a peaceful tribe, but if another tribe had interpreted the Clatsops' peaceful ways as a sign of poor fighting skills, the other tribe would have been in for a big surprise. The Clatsops had a wonderful place to reside, with a bountiful amount of seafood and berries.

CHAPTER 5

1980s

———

WHEN A TOWN DEPENDS ON tourism for its main industry but the tourists aren't showing up, something must be done. That is the position this small beach town found itself in at the end of the 1970s and beginning of the 1980s. Broadway had become dirty: parking meters were leaning over, and broken curbs and some stores looked as if they could use a face-lift. The town looked shabby and un-kempt. It was attracting the wrong type of tourists, not the desired families.

Almost anywhere in town, an individual could hear remarks like, "This is the dirtiest town I have ever been in" or "Let's go to another place for our vacation." The leaders took note and focused their atten-tion on the problem of appearance—it was time for a complete over-haul. If the town was going to survive, it needed to become a pleasant, hospitable, and inviting place in which to vacation.

In 1971 and 1972, Byron Meek and Warren Kan, presidents of the Chamber of Commerce, had each tried to foster improvements in the town. Both had failed due to inadequate financial planning. However, the time for procrastination was over; a way needed to be found to finance the redevelopment of Broadway.

A new study was made by the City Council to support the re-building. Many of the innovative ideas promoted underground services for street lighting, electrical circuits for merchants' lighting during Christmas and promotional events, enclosures where people could sit and rest, drinking fountains, and colored brick paving for intersections and crosswalks. The cost of rebuilding Broadway would be close to $1,300,000.00.

A plan was implemented, and the project started in September 1982 and was completed in May 1983. Not everyone in town favored the idea on rebuilding Broadway; some residents felt that doing so would bring too many people into town, which would dissolve the feeling of living in a small town. A strong business core was needed, and this was the way to accomplish the task.

There was so much to be accomplished—would this town be up to the task? Meetings were held with the civic leaders and the city council. All persons were free to give their input on this major development. A vibrant, strong, downtown business area was essential to the entire town. Everyone would benefit by this transition. Shopping would be easier for the local people. When the tourists came into town, the town would be welcoming.

So the work began. Contracts were written and signed. Construction started. Additional parking was one of the main concerns of the business owners. Unless the visitors could park their cars, they certainly were not going to go into the stores and shop.

It had been a tradition for young people (and sometimes older ones) to cruise Broadway. Although it was great fun to drive up and around the turnaround—sometimes two or three times—such habits did not promote shopping at the businesses. The town had always been a one-street place, but now it was time to expand the business locations to Avenue A and First Street. By the end of 1988, the design had been extended to include the two streets adjacent to Broadway. This not only increased the size of downtown, but it relieved some of the traffic problems.

There were other improvements. Downing Street, between Ocean Way and Broadway, was closed to vehicle traffic and turned into a walking street. Landscaping was done, with small resting places for the people to sit and enjoy their lunch or just rest. It has proved to be a very popular spot in town.

Broadway was closed during most of the renovation, and this did present a hardship to the town. Some businesses had a difficult time holding on during that period, but these businesses seemed to realize how much nicer the entire area would be when all renovation was finally completed.

Another major addition to the town was the Quatat Marine Park, named for the Clatsop Native American settlement on the Necanicum River. It is a riverfront park, situated on both banks of the river in the heart of downtown. It includes seating for band concerts, walkways, boat docks, and restrooms.

At the marine park, visitors can sit and watch the river lazily go by or rent paddle boats to take an enjoyable ride on the river from Avenue U to Twelfth Street. If an individual paused to watch all the aquatic activity, he or she would see many canoes, row boats, and kayaks. There is nothing more pleasant on a warm, sunny day than to sit by the river and feel the nice breeze. A delightful way to spend a summer afternoon.

The Prom was very unique to the town. Its design, with an open portal at the base, was in need of repair. As this was one of the most distinctive walkways, the structure was checked thoroughly and all needed work was completed. Now that all the improvements were made to the town, it was ready to receive visitors.

After all of the updates, new businesses were moving into town and some of the established businesses were enlarging and remodeling their shops. Restaurants such as Dooger's and Pig 'N Pancake were enlarging their space to accommodate more people.

Granderson's moved to a new location, Ter Har's expanded, and Heritage Square opened with spaces for twenty new businesses. The town was growing.

Finally it was done. So what should be done when a major project is finished? Why, throw a party!—and that is exactly what the town did. On Saturday, May 7, 1983, a dedication for the remodeling of the business district, complete with ribbon-cutting ceremonies, marching bands, and the Air National Guard flying over. Hot rods and Corvettes cruised Broadway. Hot dogs and cokes were served, and everyone had a grand time. Now the town looked like a lovely place to spend a few days and enjoy everything that was offered.

New motels and shopping malls were opened. Some of the older businesses and motels gave their places a face-lift. It was surprising what a new coat of paint could do to a tired-looking building. Everything was looking nice and fresh. People coming to town were amazed to see what this town had accomplished in such a short time.

When the Burlington Northern Railway planned to terminate service from Astoria to Seaside, the corner of Broadway and Highway 101 became available as a building site. This was at the entrance to the main part of the town and the way to the beach. It was imperative this location be used to its greatest potential.

After a survey of the merchants and the community, the decision was to move Chamber of Commerce to this very advantageous location. With a modern building and large signage, people would be informed as to the many possibilities of the town. Seaside needed to have the traffic travel to the heart of town.

Once again, a very unique partnership was formed between the Chamber, the Seaside School District, and the city. The School District received the deed to the property, leased it to the City, and the Chamber agreed to improve the property and construct an appropriate facility.

For individuals who wished to participate in the new building, they could purchase a brick for fifteen dollars, have their name engraved upon it, and then it would be placed in the entrance to the Chamber building. The rock-engraving activity was very successful, and the building was started in 1982 and completed in 1983. Again, the spirit of the town was shown; through successful cooperation, another project to enhance the town had been completed. In August 1992, the Seaside Chamber of Commerce received accreditation from the US Chamber of Commerce. This was quite an honor for a small town.

Now that Broadway was completed, people started looking around to see what other projects needed fixing or repairing. The old City Hall had been originally built in1926 and was in desperate need of an overhaul. There was no handicapped access, and the lighting and ventilation was definitely outdated. This was a project worth undertaking. Plans were drawn up, and construction began in 1989, with the staff moving to their new location in January 1990. The project was a major improvement in design and function.

The old fire station had seen better days and could not adequately accommodate all the new trucks and equipment needed for the safety of the town. A new building was started in 1989. When completed, it was nine thousand square feet in size, with five truck bays, administrative offices, and living quarters for firemen. It sat adjacent to the new City Hall.

The police station was next to be improved. The expansion consisted of five thousand square feet, interior remodeling, and a new two-story building. The expansion also included new jail facilities and quarters for officers to change clothes and workout.

The town had every reason to feel quite proud of itself. All of the new remodeling and improvements helped present a very clean, updated, modern place to reside and visit.

However, a problem seemed to be lurking under the surface. Would the city take note of this insidious problem before it was too late? Only time would tell.

CHAPTER 6

1990s

———

AT THE ANNUAL GOAL-SETTING SESSION, held by the City Council, it was decided to erect a statue of Lewis and Clark in the city. After reviewing several sketches, Stanley Wanlass's design was chosen as the winner. Grants were written and money was raised to allow the statue to be built. The total cost of the sculpture would be $95,000. One of the fund-raising events was offered by the artist. He donated an automobile sculpture entitled "Santa's New Toy" to be raffled off. The Pacific First Bank was the winner, and the sculpture was proudly displayed in the bank's lobby for everyone to see and enjoy.

On November 17, an unveiling ceremony was held at the turn-around. The statue was made of bronze and six feet high, and the base was three feet high and four feet in diameter, sitting on a concrete pad. It also depicts Captain Lewis's dog, Seaman, lying at their feet. An amazing, brilliant piece of work. Whenever a person is driving around the turnaround, he or she can see visitors having their picture taken in front of the sculpture.

A town is judged not only by its business and entertainment centers, but by its educational resources. A modern library is essential to the growth of any city. The Seaside Public Library had been adjacent to the old fire station. It was small, and more or less hidden in that building. It was time for a new library.

As the library is part of the city of Seaside, a complete expansion and remodeling program was called for. With a new building, the library had doubled its circulation and patron list. Many other services are offered, such as being able to order books for other libraries at no charge to the client. Computers are available for use as well.

In 1993, the business owners on Broadway felt they needed an organization that would promote their shops on Avenue A, Broadway, and First Avenue. As a result, the Seaside Downtown Development Association (SDDA) was formed. This has been an extremely successful organization in meeting its goal.

They sponsor four events a year. Three are car shows: Hot Rod Classic, Wheels and Waves, and Muscle and Chrome. The fourth event is the Downtown Wine Walk. In spring of each year, just before the visitors start coming to town, the SDDA promotes the hangingto of beautiful flower baskets on Broadway. Business owners contribute to this activity yearly, and its maintenance. It has also sponsored walking tours of the gardens along the main street with Master Gardner Pam Fleming. The organization has proved its value through its contributions to the town and the local businesses.

While all was going well on the surface, there still lurked the problem of congregations of idle young people during spring break, which could escalate into trouble for the town. Of course, most of these youths coming from high schools and colleges for their spring breaks were nice, proper, polite people. However, it doesn't take much to get people stirred up—just a few beers, some trash talk, and boredom can lead to a disaster, as was the case in 1962. The town was committed to preventing another disturbance of that type.

The City Council were aware of the potential problem and appointed a Spring Break Committee. It consisted of a Council member,

Seaside Police Chief, Clatsop County Sheriff, head of the county's Oregon Liquor Commission, business owner, Chamber of Commerce member, the Sunset Empire Parks and Recreation District, and a motel owner. The meetings were opened to the public and all were welcomed to give their opinions.

The committee's first assignment was to walk through downtown on Friday evening of Spring Break to get a feel of whatever was going on. It was an eye opener: the streets were lined six deep with young people who just seemed to be idly hanging out, starting a few scuffles, and yelling insults at passing cars. In certain places, the committee members could hardly walk on the sidewalk because of the large number of youths.

The scene had been crowded all week, but the weekend was definitely going to get worse. Oregon's schools took their spring break first and then Washington schools had there break. On this weekend, the town had youths from both states congregating here. It was too much for a police force comprising seventeen men to handle. Something had to be done before the next spring break to prevent the town from being taken over.

The first order of the day for the committee was to organize activities for the youths, in an attempt to keep them busy. The decision was made to close Broadway to vehicle traffic but open it to games. Sunset Empire Parks, under the direction of Mary Blake, put together a slate of fun games for all to enjoy. They included mud wrestling on the beach, rock climbing, and rolling a gigantic beach ball down Broadway.

The Oregon Zoo provided a petting exhibition and set up a display on the main street. As most of the zoo's reptiles were generally kept in controlled-temperature settings, it was a shock for some of them to be in cold weather. However, none of the animals suffered any severe consequences.

One of the most popular events was the car show. Most young men were quite proud of their vehicles and customized them. An area was roped off at the middle school, and all individuals with modified automobiles were invited to participate. Several categories were arranged for judging, such as "How Low Can You Go: How Big Is The Motor?" and "How Loud Is Your Stereo?" Members of the committee walked along Broadway and stopped cars and asked the drivers to join the competition. The police also extended invitations to many young people.

After the car was judged in the various categories, each owner was asked to turn up the stereo for one minute so the judges could hear. How they loved this part of the competition. Usually they were asked to turn it down, but now they were able to show off their invented work.

At the end of the judging, all participants were invited to the school building, where prizes were handed out. Many of the gifts had been donated by the local merchants and were gladly received. It seemed to be a success, but only time would tell.

Besides event planning, there were two other serious problems that the committee needed to address. After a long and sometimes hard winter, most motels were eager to rent rooms. This was one of the main problems in town. Parents would call motels, arrange a room for their families, pay with a credit card, and then send only the youths to occupy the room. According to the fire code, a room could only be occupied by three or four people—but suddenly ten or twelve people would be crammed into the space. Sometimes, by the time the week was over, there would be severe damage done to such heavily occupied rooms. In these cases, motel owners would have to face the expenses in repairing these accommodations.

The Spring Break Committee met with hotel and motel owners and suggested that if the parents did not show up with the youths, the motel owners could refuse the youths' requests for their rooms and return their money. Most owners complied with this request and informed the parents upon the initial telephone calls of this new procedure.

The other problem was alcoholic beverages available to young people. Some obtained liquor by doing shoulder-taps in parking lots. Youths would approach citizens over twenty-one years old and ask them to purchase beer or wine. This tactic was left for the Oregon Liquor Control Commission (OLCC) to handle. Plainclothes officers sat in cars and watched for this alcohol purchasing and immediately stepped in to catch the offenders. However, with all the precautions taken, somehow the youths still managed to secure beer and wine.

Before Spring Break began, the OLCC held classes on how to spot fake IDs. Bars were checked regularly for proper identification with the patrons. A bar owner was in serious trouble if caught serving someone under age and would be in jeopardy of having his liquor license suspended for a period of time. If too many complaints were charged against him, he might lose his license permanently.

Police officers and gang task members were in town during these two weeks. The State Police were called in to patrol the town with their dogs. With the amount of law enforcement, it looked like it a police state. Not exactly the image the town wanted to project. There was hesitancy in reducing the number of police officers. Experience had taught them that even the smallest incident could set off a full-blown disturbance.

During the daylight hours, things seemed fine, with young people playing on the beach. However, once the sun went down, then all they seemed to do was congregate on the street corners and shout insults at cars driving by.

During the winter months, the committee went to work trying to solve the problem. Would they be able to come up with a solution for this problem that was plaguing the small town? Were more police officers the answer? No one really seemed to know what resolution was needed. They realize that something had to be done.

In March 1999, all three local television stations were in town, hoping to catch something for the evening news. On the evening of March 22, a film crew was taking pictures of a large bonfire on the beach. With some encouragement from the television crew, the young people started acting up. Suddenly, they attacked the restrooms below the turnaround, ripping out toilets and wash basins and throwing them on the bonfire. During the vandalism, the film crew were rolling their cameras, cheering the vandalism on.

It is noteworthy to report that many of the young people left the beach rather than participate in destruction of public property. As the tide came in, all of the youths were forced to leave the beach, and they congregated on the turnaround. The fire department was called and they quickly doused the bonfire.

With an abundance of alcohol in these young people's systems, they became braver and more destructive. The police called for backup and it arrived. The situation had become explosive, and the rioters began marching down Broadway, smashing windows and doors of the many shops, looting merchandise along the way.

The vandalism developed into a full-scale riot, no longer a minor disturbance. The police stood firm and met the mob at the corner of Columbia and Broadway. There the rioters were asked to disperse. When they failed to obey, the police used smoke on them.

In total, two police officers were injured, and fifty young people were arrested and charged with disturbing the peace, vandalism, and looting. The film crew, who played a major role in the affair, turned over its pictures to the police department, and it was suggested they leave town.

All of the time and effort the Spring Break Committee had put into this project seemed to be futile. With encouragement from the people of the town and the City Council, they met shortly after this unfortunate incident and renewed their commitment to solve the problem.

What more could they do? How could they arrive at a solution that would meet the needs of the residents, the business owners, and the visitors who wanted to feel safe and secure when coming to town?

One of the answers was already in the works. The vacant lot that had housed the old natatorium building had been purchased by a large corporation. In addition to the lot, it purchased the two houses adjacent to this site. Their plans were to construct a 269 time-sharing unit on the site. When completed, this would bring families to town all year around. The building was finished in the 2000s and was filled every year. With so many families vacationing in town, the young people quickly found other places to go for their spring break activities. The committee was in existence until 2006, serving as the Seaside Public Safety Committee.

A new version of a very old sport was arriving, which would be ideal for the town. With the wide beach and breeze always blowing, what could be better than flying a kite? Suddenly, this market sprang to life. New stores sprouted up in the town. Kite sales soared, and store owners were extremely happy.

These were not the kites of the old days. They came in all sizes, shapes, characters, and colors. Team flying was the latest invention of the sport. The town quickly organized a kite-flying exhibition on the beach. What a sight it was. Under a brilliant blue sky, the colorful and high-flying kites danced through the air, their flights choreographed to music. The exhibition was an outstanding success.

Flying kites was an activity that could be done winter, spring, summer, and fall. Age was not an issue when competing in this sport. All it took was a bit of coordination and an imagination to make the most fanciful kite possible. In today's bright summer days, people may still watch kites hovering over the beach. There are fewer kite stores in town, but purchasing a kite and spending a day on the sand is great fun.

Many towns along the coast hold sand castle contests, another extremely popular event friendly to families. This competition is highly competitive. The designs are constructed out of wet sand and defy the imagination. Some may take as long as four or five hours to complete. Once the judging is finished, spectators have the opportunity to walk among the sculptures until the tide comes in. All spectators can do is watch as the waves gently wash away hours of preparation and work.

The 1990s was an extremely sad time for the town. They lost two of their most important citizens. Both would be extremely hard to replace.

John West had been the police chief from 1973 to 1994. He had resigned from this position and was in the fight of his life with cancer. He lost the battle and passed away. The town mourned for him. He had been a popular police chief, one who was fair and just. He treated everyone with respect but would come down hard on offenders of the law. The town trusted that the City Manager would find a replacement with all of the same qualities that had made Chief West so special.

On August 31, 1997, while most of the world was in shock over the death of Princess Diana, the town learned of the death of Bob Chisholm. Bob was head of the Seaside Public Works Department and a volunteer fireman for Gearhart. On that day, the volunteer fire department had been called to do an ocean rescue, and while swimming, Bob had suffered a heart attack and passed on. He was an extremely popular city employee and well-liked by everyone. He was especially remembered for his infectious laughter and wide grin. The Community Center now proudly bears his name in its title: The Bob

Chisholm Center. Both men were buried with full honors according to their positions. These were great losses for the town, individuals who would be hard to replace.

CHAPTER 7

2000S

THE TOWN REALIZED THAT IT needed a new, larger, and better-equipped library. In August 2008, the building was finished. It is a magnificent structure. There are special rooms for different age groups. A large children's room is stocked with books appropriate to their age. There are a youth section, a young adult section, and a Multilanguage section. Also, adequate computers are available for members and visitors.

As so many residents wanted to contribute financially to this new project, a way was found for this to be possible. It was announced that individual tiles could be purchased with family names. These tiles were then placed around the walls to the entrance of the library. Many inhabitants have lasting memories of family members who have passed on.

An individual walking through the building will certainly notice the comfortable chairs for sitting and reading. One of the most popular spots to sit and browse through the newspaper is in front of the fireplace. What could be better on a rainy day? It is indeed a welcome addition to the community.

The Friends of the Library have a section where patrons can purchase used books. All proceeds from these sales are donated to future upkeep and the purchasing of new materials.

In 2001, the cruise ships started arriving at the Port of Astoria, providing an excellent opportunity for the towns to increase their tourism businesses. Sundial Travel started to conduct tours for the passengers. Today, buses are secured to take the visitors on shopping tours of Seaside and Cannon Beach, on the Ultimate Coast Tour, Historic Astoria, Fort Stevens and Fort Clatsop, and many other important places. Many of the passengers are from foreign countries and love seeing what the coast has to offer. This has been a boost to the economy of the towns.

Many of the older places have been torn down and new buildings are being constructed in their places.

The two drug stores that had been on the corners of Holliday and Broadway have disappeared. In their place is a lovely bookstore, Beach Books, and across the corner is a Japanese restaurant.

The aquarium still stands in its original location and is now operated by great grandchildren of the original owners. There are activities for children and an educational introduction to many of the exhibits. The seals bark for their dinner and perform tricks. The general manager, Keith Chandler, is one of the few people authorized to rescue and save stranded baby seals and other mammals who have washed up on the beach. It is still one of the most popular tourist attractions in town.

New and excellent restaurants can be found on Broadway and the Prom. During the clamming season, visitors partake in eating the best fried razor clams on the coast. Chefs have been instructed on how to fix them to perfection.

The town boasts a new City Hall, Chamber of Commerce, fire station, and police station. Currently there is little serious crime in the city. The police department boosted its force to nineteen officers. A few youngsters get a little rowdy during the summer, but everything is kept under control by the efficient police force.

The fire department practices its drills every week. The force is still staffed by dedicated men and women who volunteer their time. Besides adding many new pieces of fire equipment, the fire department has brought on EMTs to assist local residents and tourists. During the summer months, when traffic is quite heavy, two EMTs may be seen riding bicycles around the town. This provides assistance in the event that someone needs help.

The 1936 fire engine, which was purchased new in that year, is used for parades and historical events. Many visitors stop by the station to have their pictures taken with the antique machine.

The department is supported by a bond issue that the citizens gladly passed. During the summer, the men and women hold an open house. There is an auction with items donated by the local merchants and private citizens. Hot dogs and hamburgers are grilled to perfection by the staff and enjoyed heartily by the citizens. Due to their excellent record, the town enjoys a great rating with the insurance industry.

Change is inevitable, sometimes good and sometimes not so good. The town fights hard to keep many of its older homes intact and lists them on the historical register. Townspeople or visitors can still take a stroll on the Prom in the evening and gaze at many of the old yet stately dwelling places. There is no uniform style to these gracious dwellings, and each one is unique. After enjoying the architecture of these buildings, an individual may choose to sit on one of the benches and regard the sunset, glimpsing glorious colors, watching the sky change from blue to pinks and reds. If an individual thus situated is lucky, he or she may even see a green flash during the sun's setting into the Pacific Ocean.

The 2000s saw increased business, tourism, and a couple of bumps in the road. Once again, the town would show its spirit of goodwill and cooperation.

In 2005 and 2006, the town lost all of its electricity for a week. Both cases occurred in the dead of winter, replete with cold days and nights. When it became evident that all power would be out for a while, many restaurants took their frozen food to the community center, which had a generator. All food was put to good use.

Hot coffee, breakfast, lunch, and dinner were served to all residents and visitors of the town at no cost. The center was flooded with volunteers who were willing to pitch in and help. It was a welcome place to go, where neighbors could sit and visit with each other.

Children could watch television or play games while enjoying peanut and jelly sandwiches. Coming together in this manner to assist all of the residents was a typical habit of the town.

Once the electricity was restored, business opened again, and people were grateful to be working again.

On the memorial weekend of 2010, an elderly gentlemen, accompanied by his granddaughter, slowly walked along Broadway. A former member of the army, he had been stationed at Fort Stevens during World War II. What's more, he could remember the evening the Japanese submarine attacked the fort. He took great pleasure in describing to his granddaughter all of the adventures he had been through. His granddaughter felt she was very fortunate to listen and vowed to remember everything her grandfather had told her.

For him, his reminiscence is a trip back in time. Although little was familiar to the gentlemen, he pointed out certain locations he remembered, such as Daley's Dairy, the record shop, Kan's Chinese restaurant, and Leonard's Saltwater Taffy. For a few pennies, a person could purchase a small bag of wonderful taffy and sit on the Prom and look out at the ocean. Suddenly, he paused where the Bungalow Dance Hall had been—the place where he had spent many Saturday evenings dancing with the local young ladies.

They sat on one of the benches, and he closed his ears to all the sounds around him and listened intently. Yes, he could hear the strains of a big band playing "In The Mood." What a delightful remembrance. In that instance, a young lady appeared in his vision, wearing a Pendleton plaid skirt, white blouse, matching cardigan sweater, and Armishaw saddle shoes with bobby socks. As she waved to her friend, the street lamp caught the reflection of her charm bracelet. Arm in arm, the young ladies entered the dance hall, and two servicemen immediately asked them to dance. They danced the night away to all the big band music.

The gentleman slowly shook his head to clear the pleasant memories. His granddaughter offered her arm in assisting him to stand up, but he doesn't need any help: those pleasant recollections have renewed his spirit. With a smile on his face, a brightness in his step, he continued his walk with his granddaughter.

Yes, those were innocent days. The town appreciates all it has had in its past and is looking forward to a bright and prosperous future. It has gone from a beach resort village, only open for three months of the year, to a pleasing family place in which to reside. Business is good all year long. Very few merchants on Broadway close their shops during the winter months. The sights and sounds of the town have changed. Old places have been torn down; new businesses have sprung up. However, certain constants have endured: the spirit, determination, love, and purpose within this wonderful location still exists in "A Town Called Seaside." The End.

EPILOGUE

THE WRITING OF THIS BOOK is a labor of love. It has been a joy to revisit my memories of the past. My family moved to Seaside in the late 1930s, and I attended grade school and high school in this town. After college, my family moved away, and outside of returning for high school reunions every five years, I was away from my beloved town.

In 1989, I made the decision to return to Seaside, where I have been happily living ever since. There have been so many changes here, but through them all, the spirit of the town has remained intact. It is still possible to walk into town and greet so many friends. The delightful shopkeepers are always willing to take a few minutes and exchange greetings with you.

Many of the people who were instrumental in rebuilding the town are now gone and sorely missed. Carl Hertig, Warren Kan, Bryon Meek, Harold Johnson, Ken Grant, and Chief John West, just to name a few. Their contributions to this town are immeasurable. However, there are new people stepping up to the plate, willing to devote hours to public and community service.

In February 2016, Seaside was pulled into the present world in a way that was unthinkable. Sergeant Jason Gooding, a member of the Seaside Police Force, was shot and killed while serving a warrant. He was the first police officer to be killed in the line of duty. Once again, everyone came together in a way that was so characteristic of a small town that had lost one of its outstanding citizens. While the entire community grieved for this loss, the heart of the town poured forth love, compassion, and aid to the widow and two small children.

The town is no longer just about summer tourists. Many visitors come in the winter to do storm and whale watching. There is a magnetic pull to watching the power and majesty of the waves, as they break over the cove's rocks on a stormy day.

In the summer on the fourth of July, visitors may watch one of the best fireworks shows, which is put on by the Chamber of Commerce and many of the businesses. During August, visitors can watch the pro-am volley ball tournament on the beach. Later on in the month, the largest relay race ever takes place. The runners start at Mt. Hood and ends up on the beach at Seaside. A total of 196 miles.

The town is still growing and becoming better and better each year. If people are seeking a vacation at one of the finest beaches in Oregon, they should consider visiting Seaside, where they will enjoy the many pleasures of small-town hospitality and fun.

ABOUT THE AUTHOR

GLORIA STIGER LINKEY, SEACOVE PUBLISHERS, moved back to her hometown after spending forty years in the insurance industry.

Linkey received as associate's degree in business administration. She now works as an adjunct instructor at Clatsop College, where she teaches publishing and marketing. Linkey is also a historian, speaker, author, and tour guide. She is proud of her little town of Seaside and is very well versed in its history.

Linkey has written two other books: *Native American Women: Three Who Changed History* and *Abby Rescues Animals*. She has two daughters and a rescue cat.